Preparing to Write and Publish Your Book:

Tips and Tricks for the Writer

by Regina (Wilkens) Yuill

Preparing to Write and Publish Your Book: Tips and Tricks for the Writer

Attention Copyright Owner:
Regina Yuill
1400 Lake Edge Court
Hoffman Estates, IL 60192

ISBN: 978-1-7335786-0-8

Library of Congress Control Number: 2019900154

Printed in the United States.

DEDICATION

Mom – thank you for being my genealogy buddy and traveling partner on all of our genealogy adventures. I am looking forward to our next adventure!

Dad – thank you for being supportive during mom and my genealogy pursuits.

John Yuill – for letting me take over one whole room in our house just for my genealogy.

And to **all my ancestors** who came before me and left a trail for me to follow.

TABLE OF CONTENTS

TABLE OF FIGURES

TABLE OF TABLES

FOREWORD

I have been doing genealogy since 1987 and never thought I would write a book about my maternal family history let alone writing and publishing a guidebook about the writing and publishing process.

The concept for a family history book began many years ago after my mother and I went on several genealogy adventures. After researching and gathering the family history in the United States, one such genealogy adventure for Mom and me came when we decide to jump "over the Pond" to Ireland.

In September 2001, my mother and I boarded a plane to Ireland in order to research our Irish ancestors. We visited several repositories in Dublin and County Cavan. While in County Cavan we were able to find the cottage our ancestors' lived in and where they farmed. After gathering the Irish documents and a piece of a stone from our ancestors' cottage (yes, we brought a part of the cottage home with us!), we started discussing ways to share and preserve the genealogy records so other family members could enjoy the information we found.

I suggested to Mom that a family reunion would be nice so everyone could learn the history of our Irish ancestors. We began to organize our genealogy so we could show off our finds at the reunion. In 2003, we had our first reunion and did a show and tell for the attendees, which was a huge success and generated a lot of interest in our Irish ancestors. After the attendees reviewed the information Mom and I had gathered over the years, they kept asking when the family history book would be published. In the fall of 2003 I began to write the family book and once the attendees knew I was writing the family book, they contributed their family stories and photographs, as they also wanted their family line mentioned in the book.

Little did I realize the daunting task I was about to undertake in writing the family history. From the day I started writing until the day I published the family history book in 2005, I discovered a deficiency in writing and publishing guidebooks for genealogists. I attended a lot of genealogy society meetings and national genealogy conferences, but did not find any guidebooks explaining writing and publishing steps for preparing a book. Not having experience with setting up indexes, table of contents, footnotes, endnotes, photographs and plain old writing, the process involved a lot of trial and error because of the lack of writing and publishing aids available. I was on my own!

Another interesting problem I learned while trying to write about my ancestors was the naming conventions used by my ancestors. I first started writing by combining all the ancestors together, i.e. brothers, sisters, parents all lumped together into one huge story, but quickly realized that every family unit had a Joseph, Phillip, John, Mary, Stephen, Bridget, etc., which caused a lot of "who does this Phillip or Mary belong to" consternations. A lot of head scratching and do-overs happened. I knew I had found a way to organize and sort the families in order to resolve the "who's who" issue, but I was stumped as to how to split the ancestors out.

Luckily, the *Family Chronicle* magazine had just arrived in the mailbox and "lo and behold" serendipity happened because this issue included an article from another genealogist explaining her family organization system. After reading the article, the light bulb went off and the "who's who" was resolved.

Many years later after completing my family history book, one of my genealogy clubs decided to have a "show and tell" day and of course I had to show off my book. While showing and discussing my book, which is entitled *Climbing the Irish Shamrock – Phillip and Mary (Sexton) Carolan Family History* – 1834 to 2005, I had several members ask how I had accomplished the writing and publishing task. Plus, the president of our club asked if I would give a presentation regarding the writing and publishing process. I did the presentation, but members were still struggling with their writing and publishing process and asked if I could recommend guidebooks to help them.

Well, the seed was planted and as I am a strong believer in preserving one's family history for future generations, I decided to write this guidebook. Being an analytical thinker in which step-by-step instructions help me, I wrote this guidebook in the hopes it helps fellow genealogists write and publish their books following the steps described in the book.

Good luck, have fun and I hope you write and publish your family book for others to enjoy!

ACKNOWLEDGMENTS

To **Deborah Spacko** for reading and offering feedback on this book.

To **Thomas MacEntee** for editing and mentoring me through the print-on-demand publishing techniques.

To **Joel H. Ferrin, Esq.** and **Thomas Burton, Esq.** for assisting with the contract review and copyright questions.

To **Jennie Broering** for designing a beautiful book cover.

CHAPTER 1: WHY MEDIA MATTERS

The media you choose for your book is important since media formats and outlets do change over time. Thousands of years ago our ancestors were allowed to write on their walls; try that at home now and TROUBLE awaits you! As our ancestors advanced in society, so did the media outlets they used. I often wonder what their thoughts were when newspapers, books, and electronic technology became new trends. How did our ancestors react? Did they react with fear or excitement?

I know from my own experiences I have felt excitement when a new media format was introduced, but I have also experienced fear. Remember the old DOS and WordPerfect programs used in the business world, and the fear of change you felt when Microsoft Word was then introduced! I know a few choice words probably came out of my mouth because everything was different, and I was out of my comfort zone. But once I tried it and became familiar with Microsoft Word, everything fell into place.

And remember VCR machines? Okay, I am showing my age, but I remember purchasing my first VCR machine and tapes in 1980 just so I could tape my favorite movies. Like WordPerfect, VCR machines, DVDs and CDs are so passé now as my grandchildren would say.

Media technology and formats have changed greatly in the last ten years. Some of us jumped in with both feet while some of us dragged our feet until we were forced to address the new media concepts. We all know how internet, streaming, e-books and cloud storage have changed the way we watch, read, store and retrieve our data files.

I do have to admit the current media technology has made my life simpler, since now I can access my movies, books and computer files anywhere and anytime. In addition, internet, streaming, e-books and cloud storage have eliminated clutter in my genealogy room. But I do wonder which of the abovementioned media technology will disappear and what new technology will be invented to allow us to read our old media files.

As a genealogist, I like the electronic advantages of (i) less clutter; (ii) access; and (iii) portability. As a writer I like the e-book advantages of (i) lower publishing costs; (ii) updates are easier; and (iii) portability.

But having a little bit of a realist personality, I not only understand the advantages, I also see the disadvantages. While an e-book is limited by technology, a print book is not limited by technology. History has shown that print books have longevity.[1]

And as a realist, I will be publishing this book in print and e-book formats.

CHAPTER 2: HOW TO GET STARTED ON YOUR BOOK

Compile and Organize Research

Researching, organizing, writing and publishing are the cornerstones of a book and work simultaneously together when creating such book. As you research your genealogy information, you should be thinking about the organization of your book. For example: oldest ancestor at the beginning followed by the descendants or *vice versa*. Writing a genealogy book also helps fill in research holes and possible mistakes. That is, did you miss an enter generation or did you research the wrong family?

In addition, as you research, organize and write, it is best to start searching for a publishing company that can handle your publishing needs. Whether you are using a publishing company or self-publishing, it is best to review the publishing company's printing requirements early in the writing process to avoid hiccups and do-overs.

It is also important to review and organize your genealogy documents in order to determine how you plan to use them in your book. Organizing your documents helps you figure out the scope of your book, i.e., who, what, where, when, how and why to include and/or write about certain family information.

I know firsthand how organizing your research documents helps determine research holes and missed generations. As mentioned before, I have been doing genealogy research since 1987 and my "research hole" situation occurred back in 1993. During many genealogy adventures with Mom, we had heard the family oral history and received various genealogy documents regarding an ancestor who fought in the American Revolution. After learning that we had an ancestor who fought in the Revolutionary War, I thought it would be fun to research this ancestor so we could join the National Society Daughters of the American Revolution ("DAR").

With only six years' experience in genealogy research, I thought to myself, "No problem!" I began working on my paternal grandmother's family line using the oral history and the documents received from other relatives as my starting point. Even though I received great stories and documents from others, I knew I had to verify the oral history and accuracy of the genealogy documents. Following the Board for Certification of Genealogists ("BCG") standards I discovered a big hole in the research I had received. I discovered there was a missing generation! I am not sure how my 3x great-grandfather was tagged as the Revolutionary War patriot, but when I calculated his age at death as 135 years, I knew he could not be the Revolutionary War patriot since life expectancy for persons living in the 18th century was approximately 35 years.[2]

My research finally proved who the real patriot was: my 4x great-grandfather. Once I had the proof, I found myself saying, "Will the real Revolutionary War patriot please stand" using the line from the television show *To Tell the Truth*.[3]

4x Great Grandfather	3x Great Grandfather	2x Great Grandfather	Great-Grandfather	Grandmother
Col. John Piper	John Piper	Thomas Piper	Harry Piper	Olive Piper

As mentioned above, the use of the BCG standards helped resolve the Revolutionary War patriot issue. These BCG standards, if properly followed, will help you research and will ensure that your research is accurate. The BCG standards are:

1. A reasonably exhaustive search;
2. Complete and accurate source citations;
3. Analysis and correlation of the collected information; and
4. Resolution of any conflicting evidence.

These standards can be reviewed on the Board for Certification of Genealogists website at https://bcgcertification.org. BCG explains the standards for researching, documentation, and writing. I recommend that you review the BCG page so that your book meets these standards.

Organization also saves time when writing your book, because it puts the documents at your fingertips. If you still need help with organization ideas, I would recommend checking out Thomas MacEntee's "Genealogy Do-Over" topic on his Abundant Genealogy website at https://abundantgenealogy.com. The *Genealogy Do-Over* will give you great ideas on preparing research, setting research goals, establishing good practices and guidelines, tracking research, citing sources, etc.

What Is a Target Audience?

As you compile and organize, you need to think about your Target Audience. Your target audience can affect the size of the book. It is your choice as to whom you wish to write about and include in your book. Will you write (1) an extensive family history about a specific ancestor and all his descendants; (2) a family history book about your immediate family; or (3) a history of your life events? Remember, it is your choice to go big or small when writing your story.

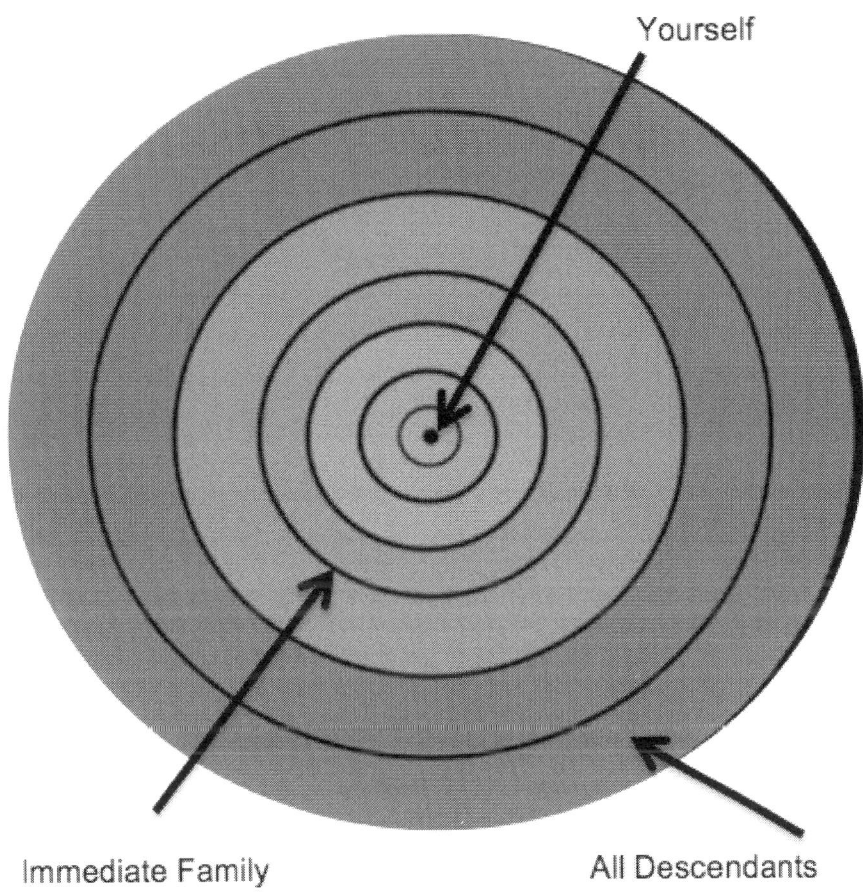

Figure 1 - Target Audience

CHAPTER 3: DETERMINING THE BOOK SIZE

There are four standard book sizes that are usually used when publishing a book and they are:

- 8.5 x 11 inches
- 7 x 10 inches
- 6 x 9 inches; and
- 5.5 x 8.5 inches

The size of the book can play a significant part in the printing cost since publishers may base the cost on the size of book and/or the number of pages in the book. For example, an 8.5 x 11 inch book with 200 pages may be a 400-page book if a 5.5 x 8.5 inch size is chosen since the amount of words on a page differs between the two sizes.

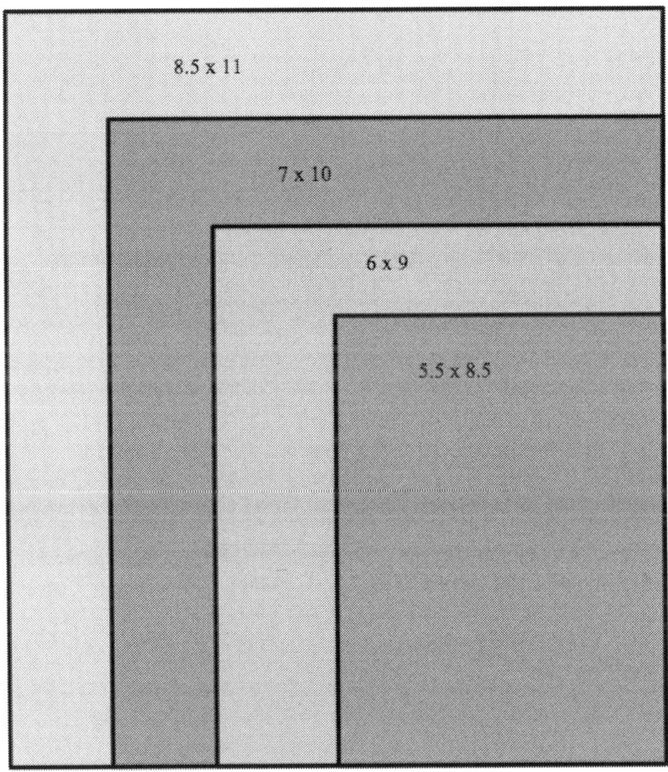

Figure 2 - Book Size

Book margins must be considered if the book is to be bound. It is important to leave adequate margin space so that the words are not cut off once the book is bound. A typical standard for margins are: (i) side margins = .75 inches; (ii) top margin = .50 inches; and (iii) bottom margin = .50 inches.

CHAPTER 4: TYPEFACE, FONT AND LEADING FORMATS

A common mistake made by writers is not picking the best typeface, font and leading (paragraph spacing) for the book. Two characteristics to keep in mind when selecting options is:

1. **Legibility**, which is the measure of clarity. Basically, how easily can one letter be distinguished from another; and
2. **Readability**, which refers to how the letters and characters interact with the composed words, sentences and paragraphs. The ease of reading plays a large role in keeping your reader's attention.

It is important to know your audience as well. Elderly or sight-impaired readers may need an enlarged or bold typeface and prefer a font such as Arial or Times New Roman; younger readers may be fine with a small and un-bolded typeface and font.

Some of the best and worst typeface and fonts for printing are:

Best Typeface (Fonts)	
Best	**Reason**
Times Roman	Good, basic choice
Futura	Clean, modern
Goudy	Elegant, reserved
Helvetica	To the point
Garamond	Easy to read
Bookman	Casual, friendly

Worst Typeface (Fonts)	
Worst	**Reason**
Comic scans	Popular in targeting kids and hard to read
Impact	Ultra thick strokes and a compressed letter structure. Very had to read
Papyrus	Consider the king of bad fonts. Equal parts childish, kitschy and irritating
Segoe Script	Not easy to read and does not complement other fonts
Brush Script	Old out of dated and can cause problems when printing
Bradley Hand	Hard to read

Table 1 - Font Pros and Cons

Typeface

Typeface is the visual appearance or style while a font is what you use. Typeface has a specific weight, style, width, slant, italicization, ornamentation and size.

Before the digital age, printers used metal letters, numbers and symbols to set the overall look of the document. For example, the printer may decide that Arial is to be the typeface used, and in choosing Arial the printer would include in his choice the bold and italic metal letters, numbers and symbols of Arial.

There are thousands of different typefaces in existence, and the digital age of computers has helped and continues to help in the development of new typefaces.

Typeface is usually chosen based upon the (1) legibility; (2) readability; (3) appropriateness for the audience and the message; (4) reproducibility; and (5) practicality. The typeface used will set the tone of your book.

Fonts

Fonts are the delivery mechanism of the typeface design and also relate to the size and variation of characters printed in a document. Fonts are the size, weight, style and color of a typeface and are measured in units called points (pt), i.e., 8 pt, 12 pt, 32 pt, 72 pt, etc. Fonts are grouped together in a family and are referred to as a font family. Usually a font family will have a minimum of 2 fonts, for example bold and italic, but there can be more, as there is no maximum limit for a font family.[4]

Typeface	Fonts (a/k/a Font Family)	12 pt
Arial	Regular **Bold** *Italic* ***Bold Italic***	abcdef **ghijklm** *nopqrs* ***tuvxyz***
Calibri	Regular **Bold** *Italic* ***Bold Italic*** Light	abcd **efghi** *jklm* ***nopqrs*** tuvxyz
Courier New	Regular **Bold** Bold Oblique Oblique	abcdef **ghijklm** nopqrs tuvxyz

Table 2 - Typeface, Fonts and Points

The font size for the normal text, index, chapter headings, photograph captions, and endnotes should be a different font size to distinguish them. Most publishing companies recommend the following font sizes:

Normal text	10 to 12 pt
Chapter headings & subheadings	Larger point size (usually 12 to 24 pt)
"Running heads" (book or chapter titles at top of every page)	Same size as text or smaller
Photo captions	1 size smaller than text
References, footnotes & indexes	2 sizes smaller

Table 3 - Fonts / Where and When to Use

Leading

Another important book setup is "leading." Leading (pronounced *led-ing*) is the vertical space between the lines of text. Leading derives from the days when newspapers and books were setup by typesetters using thin strips of lead to separate the lines. With the invention of computers and digital typesetting, the leading value now includes the size of the font, and allows you to specify the leading you wish to use. For example, a 10 pt text with 2 pts of spacing between lines would mean a leading of 12 pts.

Examples of Leading and best practices for using:

Times Roman 8 point, 10 point leading	Normally used for the indexes and/or references
Times Roman 9 point, 11 point leading	Often used for photo captions (through some people prefer to use 9 point bold italic, because it stands out better. May wish to use on running headers & page number
Times Roman 10 point, 12 point leading	Good choice if you wish to save money by fitting your text into fewer pages. Reference material does well in this point size, as do lengthy quotations or information insets
Times Roman 11 point, 13 point leading	11 point Good choice for easy-to-read, general body text. Can use 14 point leading to expand page count and make text even more readable
Times Roman 12 point, 14 point leading	People with particular concerns about readability often use 12 point with 14 or 15 point leading

Table 4 - Leading Examples

NOTE: actual size of the typeface, font and leading given above.

Steps to Setup Typeface, Font and Leading

The following instructions are given for Microsoft Word 2013, Windows Version and Microsoft Word for Mac 2011, Windows Version:

Typeface and Font

1. On the Tool Bar, select **Format**; click **Font**
2. Select the **Font**
3. Select the **Font Style**
4. Select the **Size**
5. Press **OK**

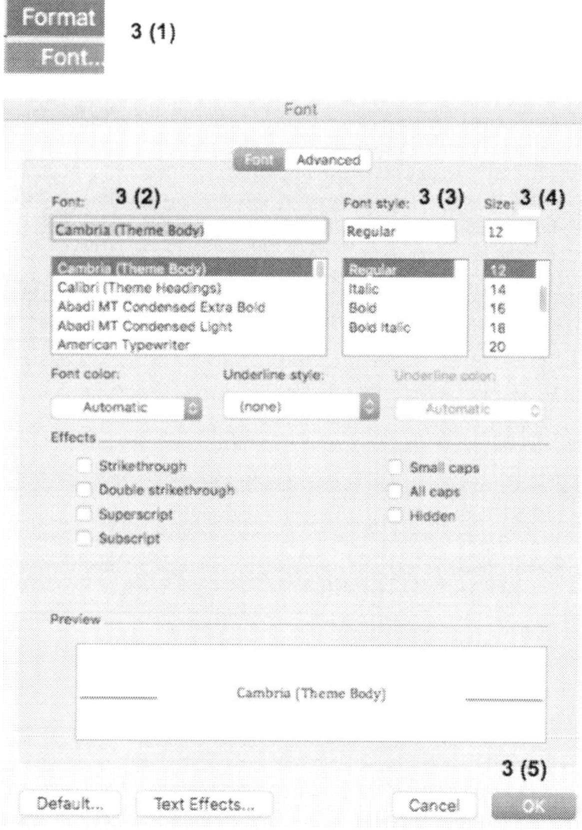

Figure 3 (1) through 3 (5) - Typeface and Font Setup

Leading Line Spacing

1. Select **Format** and then click **Paragraph**
2. The **Paragraph** dialog box appears; select **Indents and Spacing**
3. In the **Line Spacing** section, click the drop down arrow and select **Exactly**
4. Select the point (pt) size in the **At** section
5. Press **OK**

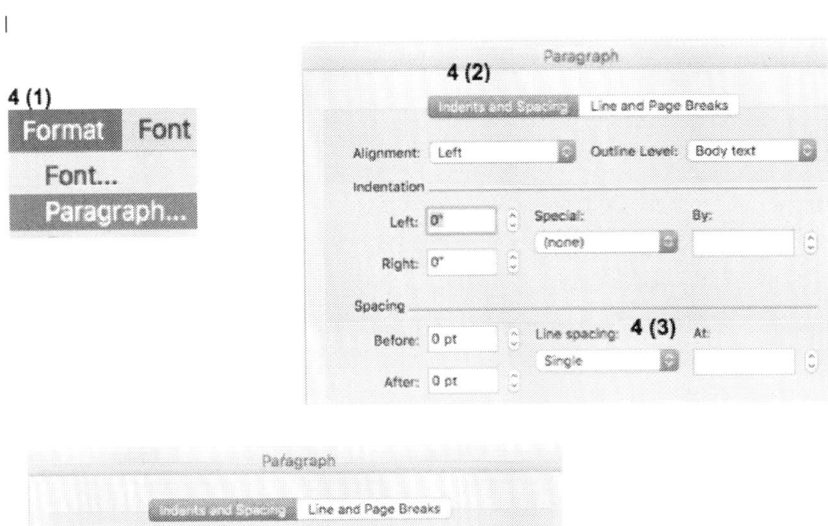

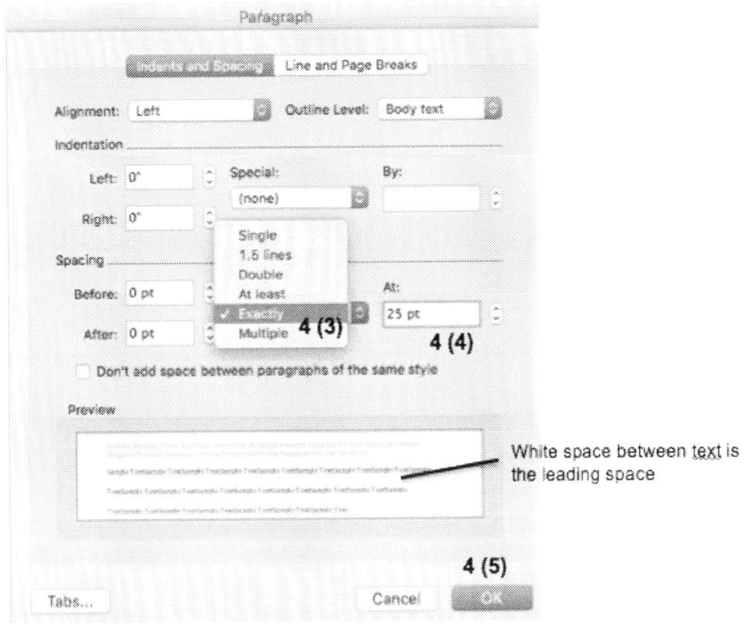

Figure 4 (1) through 4 (5) - Setup for Leading Space

CHAPTER 5: INSIDE THE BOOK

Title Page

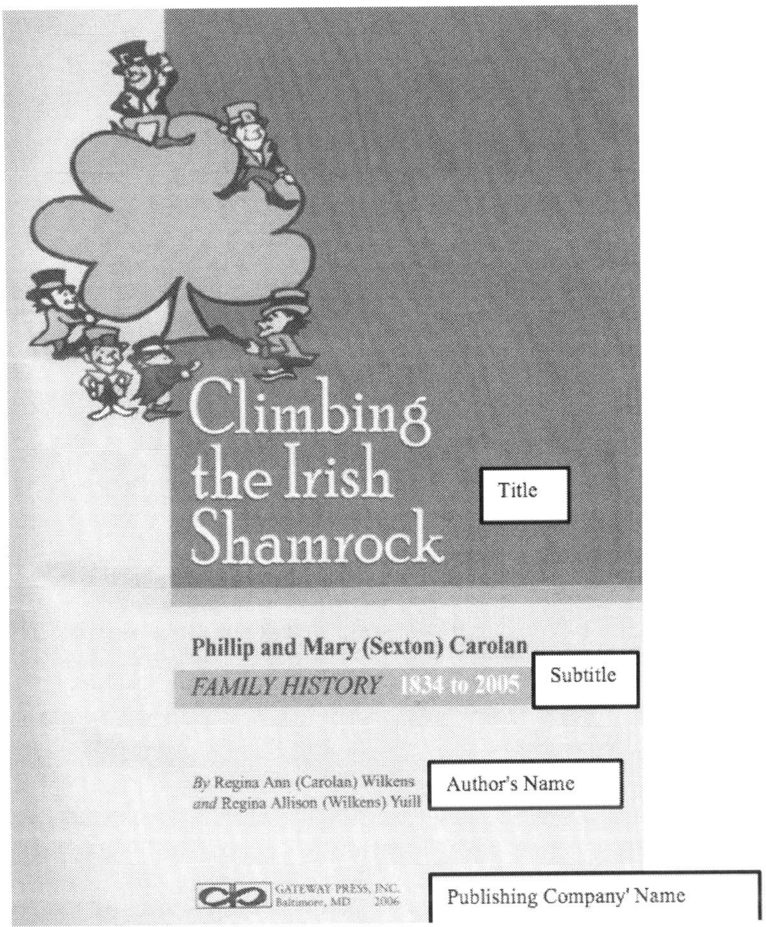

Figure 5 - Example Title Page

Intellectual Property

Intellectual Property refers to original creations of the mind, such as inventions, books, music, artistic works, designs, software, etc. Intellectual property covers: (a) patents; (b) trademark and service mark; and (c) copyright.[5]

The United States Patent and Trademark Office ("USPTO") is responsible for processing, granting and preserving trademarks, service marks, and patents issued in the United States.

Patents

If a person invents a new product, technique or process, it can be patented. The USPTO handles the issuing of a patent by examining the patent application and determining if a patent can be issued. In addition to examining and issuing a patent, the USPTO is responsible for (1) publishing, (2) distributing, (3) maintaining patent files, (4) providing copies to the public, and (5) protecting and preserving the inventors.

There are three types of patents:

a) **Utility patent** which may be granted to anyone who invents or discovers any new or useful process, machine, article of manufacture, or composition of matter, or any new and useful improvement thereof;

b) **Design patent** may be granted to anyone who invents a new, original, and ornamental design for an article of manufacture; and

c) **Plant patents** may be granted to anyone who invents or discovers and reproduces any distinct and new variety of plant.

A patent grants the right to exclude others from making, using, offering for sale, or selling the invention in the United States.

Trademark and Service Mark

Trademarks and Service Marks protect and distinguish products or services from others. A word, name, symbol, sign, design or expression capable of distinguishing products between companies and/or individuals is a Trademark.

Distinguishing trademarks are:

Figure 6 - Example of Trademark Symbols

Service Marks distinguish the services between businesses. For example, McDonald's Service Mark is its restaurant services while Wal-Mart's Service Mark is its retail store services.

Trademarks and Service Marks can be confusing. For example McDonald's, has a Trademark and Service Mark. McDonald's Trademark is the yellow "M" printed on a red background and used on its products, i.e. cups, wrappers, and signage. Another McDonald's Trademark is The Big Mac, but its Service Mark is the restaurant services it offers.

Like patents, a trademark and service mark must be registered with the USPTO in order to protect them. Trademark and Service Marks exist to protect consumers and businesses. Without clear distinguishing Trademarks or Service Marks, customers and businesses will not know who manufactured a product or who is providing the service.

Copyright

Copyright law protects original works of books, music, movies, and pictures (the "works").[6] When a copyright is established, the creator of the works has control and exclusive rights to the works. Copyright is established at the time the works is created or at the time when the works becomes visible to third parties. It is advisable to officially record the date your works was created in order to make it easier to tackle plagiarism, imitations or copies.

For works to be eligible for copyright protection the following conditions must be met:

a) It must be in the field of literature, science or art;
b) It must be original;
c) It must be recorded in particular form; and
d) It must be noticeable.

Without copyright protection, others can exploit the creator's works and can avoid paying royalties to the creator. If you are doing all the hard work, you should protect your works from others so they cannot profit from your works.

You should understand what copyright could do for you and what rights you have under the copyright laws. You should:

a) Retain the copyrights of your book;
b) Review and have a basic understanding of the copyrights law;
c) Should always give credit where credit is due;
d) Obtain permission to use other's copyright matter; and
e) Consult with an attorney or person specializing in copyright law, if in doubt.

When you prepare your copyright page for your book, it should include the following:

a) Copyright date;
b) Restrictions and permissions regarding the reproduction;
c) Author's name and contact information;
d) Library of Congress number and/or the International Standard Book Number ("ISBN");
e) Name of book;
f) Edition number of the book (ex: 1st, 2nd, 3rd);
g) Publishing company's information and address; and
h) Location where the book was printed

Preparing to Write and Publish Your Book: Tips and Tricks for the Writer
Copyright © 2018 by Regina (Wilkens) Yuill. Print edition.

All rights reserved. No part of this book may be reproduced, distributed, or transmitted in any form or by any means, including photocopying, recording, or other electronic or mechanical methods, or any other methods, including but limited to, information storage and retrieval systems or reproduction via the Internet without the prior written permission of the copyright owner, except in the case of brief quotations embodied in critical reviews and certain other noncommercial uses permitted by copyright law. For permission requests, write to the copyright owner, addressed to

Attention Copyright Owner:
Regina Yuill
1400 Lake Edge Court
Hoffman Estates, IL 60192

While all attempts have been made to verify the information provided in this publication, neither the author nor the publisher assume any responsibility for errors, omissions, or contrary interpretations of the subject matter herein.

Neither the author nor the publisher assumes any responsibility or liability whatsoever on the behalf of the purchaser or reader of these materials.

Library of Congress Cataloging-in-Publication Data is available on file.

Cover design and illustration by Jennie Broering

Print ISBN:
Ebook ISBN:

Printed in the United States

Figure 7 - Example of Copyright Page

Dedication, Foreword, Preface and Acknowledgements

Dedication

The Dedication is placed on a separate page in the front of the book and is a personal message of thanks to someone or something that inspired or helped you during the creation of your book. Most writers provide a reason for their dedication selection.

When choosing to whom to write a Dedication, think about the process you just went through and who helped you accomplish the process in writing your book. Your dedication could include a variety of people, i.e. parent(s), sibling(s), spouse, partner, friend(s), supervisor or even a favorite pet.

While most people are appropriate for the Dedication, there are times when dedicating a book to a certain person(s) is not. The books subject matter can play a part in eliminating someone. For example, dedicating a book to a child when the book deals with adult matters may be inappropriate.

Limiting the Dedication to just a couple of names is most traditional. After all, the Dedication is a high honor; dedicating a book to a lot of people tends to diminish its specialness.

Don't stress out or worry about the Dedication page right away. I did not write my dedication for my family history book, *Climbing the Irish Shamrock*, until the final draft. Waiting to write the Dedication allowed me to dedicate my book to the special person who inspired me during the writing and publishing process.

Other Dedication tips and tricks:[7]

a) Make a list of persons or things that inspired or helped you;
b) Think about the reason why you want to dedicate your book to someone;
c) Review your favorite authors publications for dedication ideas;
d) A dedication can be as simple as a "To", "For", or "In Loving Memory of";
e) Double check and have someone else read your dedication to ensure the meaning is clear and error free;

Even though you have dedicated your book to a special person you can also mention that person in the acknowledgment.

Foreword

The Foreword is placed at the beginning of the book and is usually a short piece written by someone other than the author; it gives an introduction of the book. The person writing the Foreword may be someone influential and whose credibility regarding the subject matter is well known.

The author can also write the Foreword page, and when the author writes the Foreword it usually tells the story of how the book idea developed.

If you add a Foreword to your book, you should consider: (1) the importance of the book: *what makes this book better than another and why a person should read this book?*; (2) the qualifications of the author: *does the author have experience in the subject matter written in the book?*; and (3) the value in reading the book: *does the reader gain or learn something from reading the book?*

Preface

A Preface is an introduction written by the author and is more common in non-fiction books. The Preface is a place for the author to discuss situations surrounding the book, i.e., the idea for the book, the book development, the writing and publishing processes. A Preface can be short or long. It is a place to be honest and open about the writing of your book and gives readers a chance to get to know you. Writing a book is hard work and a journey; therefore, showcase your accomplishment.

If you want to explain or clarify something about your book or writing the book, the Preface is the place to do it.

You may also wish to add a statement as to why a reader should spend time reading your book. The Preface can be a great marketing tool when trying to get your book read. The Preface page is usually signed and dated.

Acknowledgments

The Acknowledgments page follows the Preface and is placed in the front of the book after the inside cover page and the Copyright page. Or you may choose to put the Acknowledgments page before or after the Table of Contents page. The Acknowledgments page should be one page in length. A two-page acknowledgment is too long and runs the risk of making your reader lose interest. A "short and sweet" acknowledgment works best.

An Acknowledgments page allows you to thank and give credit to those persons who contributed to your book by editing, giving moral support, and publishing assistance. It is basically a way to publicly display your appreciation for their assistance and support.

There are no set rules regarding whom to include in your acknowledgement. However, most authors acknowledge: (1) family members who supported your endeavors in writing the book; (2) persons who provided research, data or case studies; (3) the editor; (4) the illustrator; (5) the designer (front and back cover design for the book); (6) a mentor who showed you the ropes; and (7) the publisher.

If you are thanking a person for their support, just saying thank you is not enough. You should list the reasons why you acknowledged the person. For example, "A special thank you to my Mom for giving me the love of genealogy, and to Dad for letting me "steal" Mom to go on our genealogy research trips". Also, don't include *too many* people in your acknowledgements for fear that someone will be left out or offended. Include those closest to you and the project—the others will understand.

Have a third-party review your Acknowledgments page before it is set in stone. Did you inadvertently leave an important person out? Is it written well? Could it be written better or condensed even further?

If you follow these guidelines, you'll have a well-written Acknowledgments page that gives credit where credit is due.

Chapter Headings for the Table of Contents

If you have organized your information, you should have a sense for your chapter headings and as you write you can set up and mark the chapter headings. For example, my chapter headings for my Wilkens Family History Book I am currently writing are:

CHAPTER 1:	**HENRY AND ELIZABETH (LAMMERS) WILKENS**		
CHAPTER 2:	**JOSEPH AND MARY (VOSTEN) WILKENS**		
CHAPTER 3:	**MARY (WILKENS) AND HENRY NEUERBURG**		
	CHAPTER 3A:	TERESA NEUERBURG	
CHAPTER 4:	**GEORGE AND CLARA (HENDRICKS) WILKENS**		
	CHAPTER 4A:	JOSEPH	
	CHAPTER 4B:	EMMA	
	CHAPTER 4C:	WILLIAM and OLIVE (PIPER)	
		CHAPTER 4C1:	HARRY
		CHAPTER 4C2:	ROBERT
		CHAPTER 4C3:	MARY LOU
	CHAPTER 4D:	VI	
		CHAPTER 4D1:	DIXIE
		CHAPTER 4D2:	TRACY
	CHAPTER 4E:	CLARA	
	CHAPTER 4F:	WALT	
	CHAPTER 4G:	EDWARD	
CHAPTER 5:	**EMMA (WILKENS) AND STEPHAN VANDERLOO**		

Example of Chapter Headings

The Chapter Headings 1, 2, 3, 4 and 5 are to the primary chapter headings while Chapter 3A, 4A through 4G are the Sub-chapters and Chapters 4C1, 4C2, 4C3 and 4D1 are Sub-sub chapter headings.

Once you have your chapter headings arranged, you will need to take the following steps to set the level and format style in order to include them in the table of contents:

1. Highlight the primary chapter headings

   CHAPTER 2: JOSEPH AND MARY (WULKOTTE) VORSTEN
   CHAPTER 3: MARY (WILKENS) AND HENRY NEUERBURG
   CHAPTER 4: GEORGE H AND CLARA (HENDRICKS) WILKENS

   Figure 8 (1) through 8 (9) - Chapter Headings Setup

2. Select **Heading 1** in the **Styles Tool Bar** section.

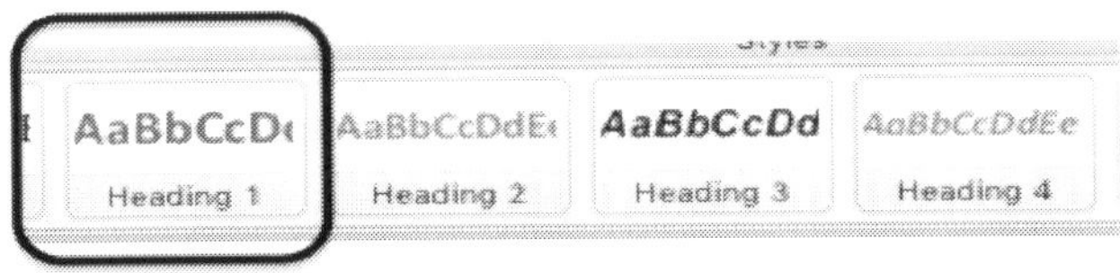

Figure 8 (2) – Heading 1

3. The next step is to choose the font style and the line spacing for your Table of Contents.

a) Select **Insert** from the Tool Bar and then select **Index and Tables**

b) In the **Index and Tables** dialog, select **Table of Contents**

c) In the **Formats** section select a **Format** style for your Table of Contents. Then preview your selection in the **Preview** section and decide which **Format** will work best with your Table of Contents; and

d) After you have chosen the **Format**, click on the **Modify** button and the **Styles** box will open.

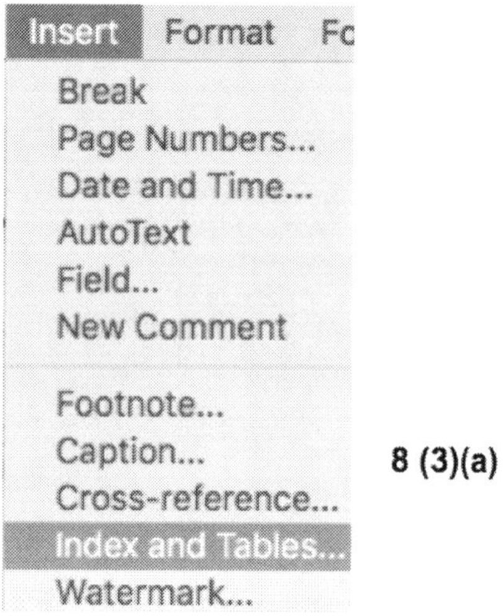

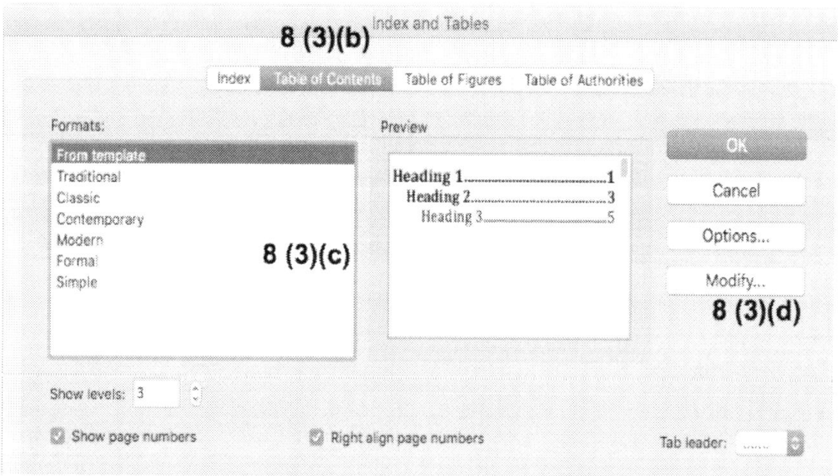

Figure 8 (1) through 8 (9) – Chapter Headings Setup

4. The **Style** section allows you to select the font, line spacing, and indentation for your Table of Content. The abbreviation "TOC#" refers to the Table of Contents heading in your book. For example, Heading 1, Heading 2, Heading 3, etc., located in the Styles Tool Bar box. Select **Modify**

Figure - 8 (4) - TOC Styles

5. After the **Modify Style** dialog box opens, review the **Properties** section to ensure that the following properties are correct:

   a) **Name** field should match the **TOC# Styles Heading** button you wish to format, e.g., Heading 1;

   b) **Style based on** field should be set to the Heading # you are modifying; and

   c) **Style for following paragraph** field should also be set to the same Heading # you selected under "Style based on".

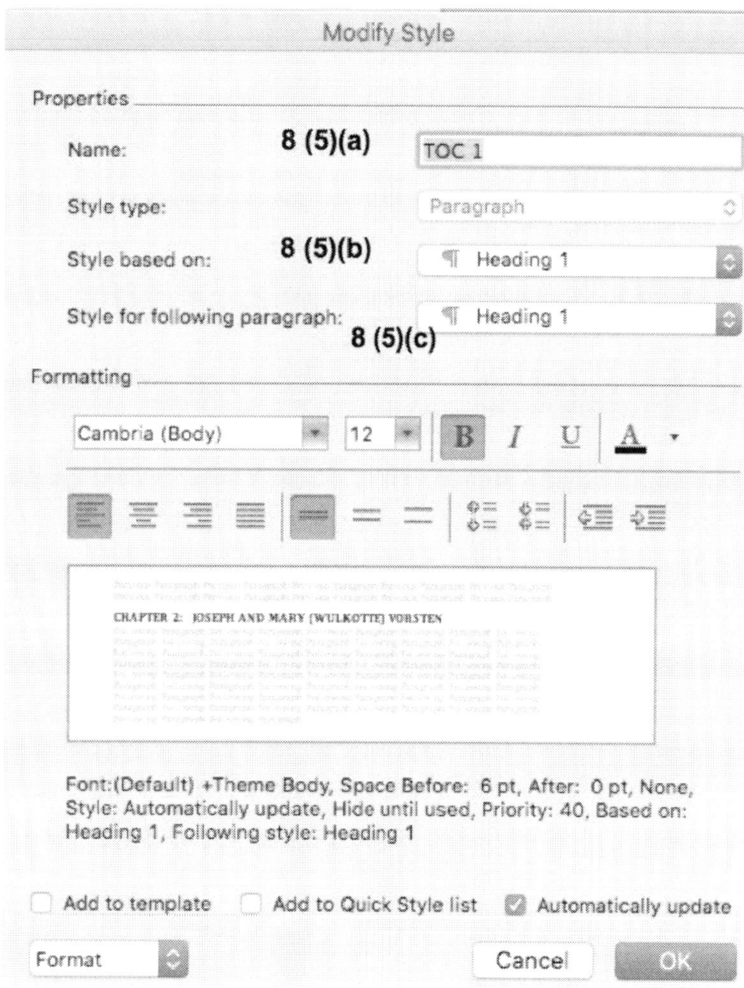

Figure 8 (5)(a) through (c) - Table of Content Style Setup for Heading 1

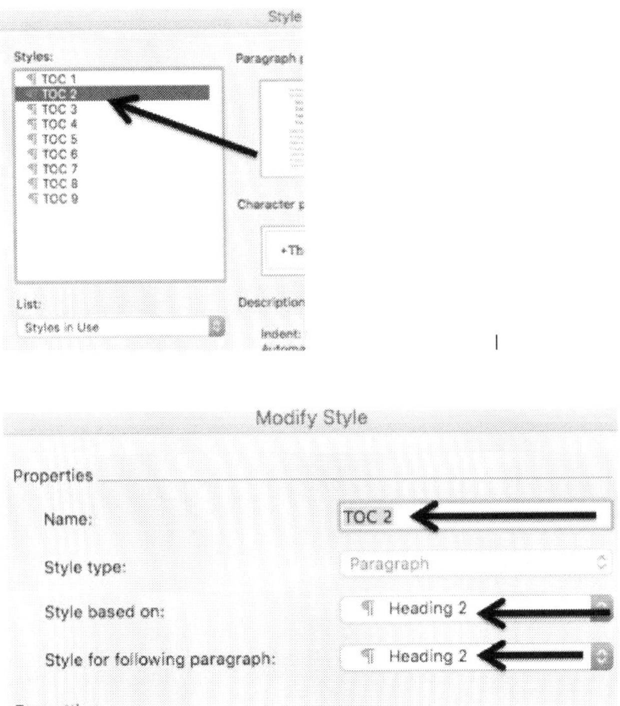

Example of Table of Content Styles Setup for Heading TOC2

6. After setting the **Properties** to the correct TOC# and Heading #, it is time to set the font, line spacing and indentation. There are two methods you can use to set the font. The first method can be handled by using the **Formatting** section:

   a) Use the drop down field to select the **Font** to use for your **Heading**; and

   b) Then use the drop down field for the **Font Size** and select the size of the font.

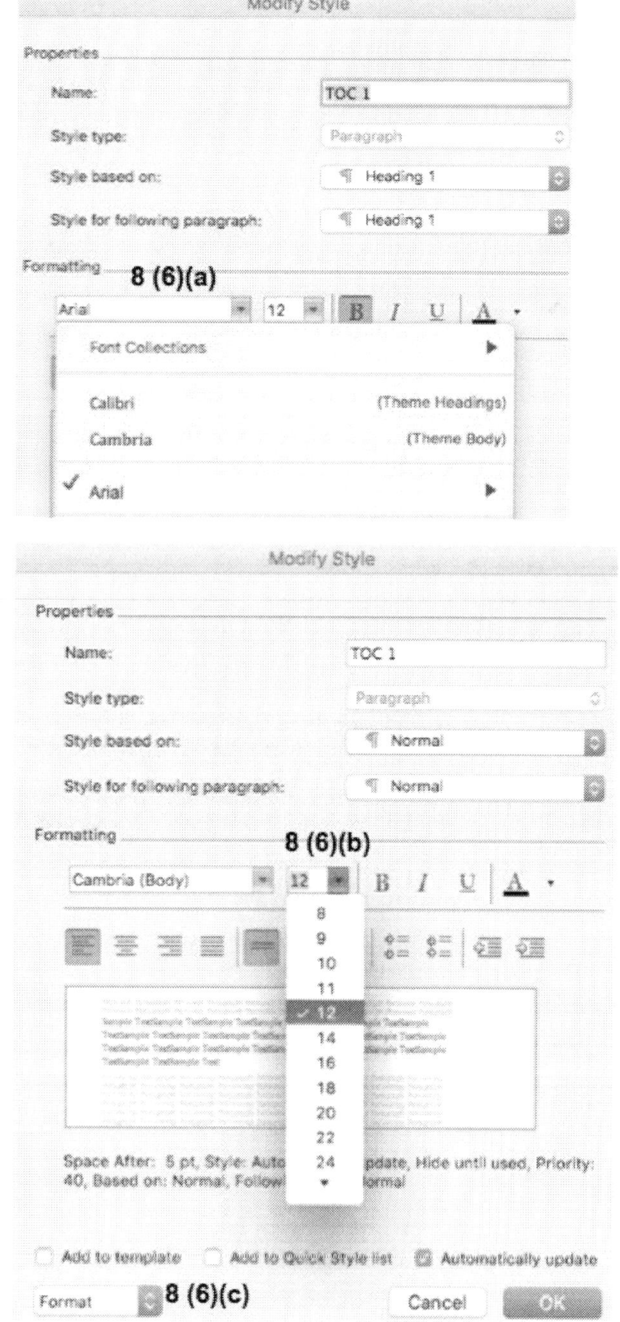

Figure 8 (6)(a), (b), and (c) - Table of Content Modify Steps

c) The second font setup method is handled by clicking the drop down arrow in the **Format** section at the bottom of the **Modify Style** dialog box (see (c) marked in the image above); and

d) Select **Font**, **Font Style** and **Font Size**.

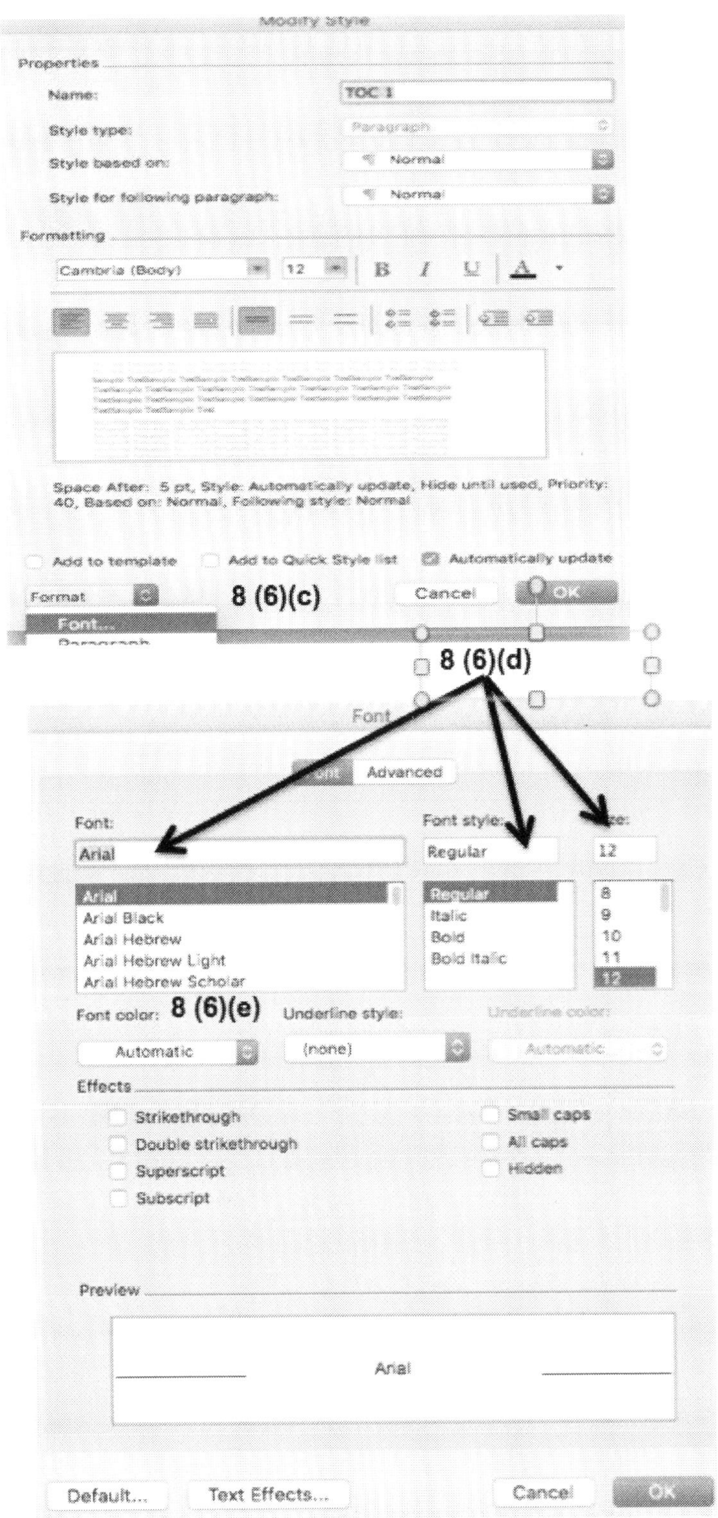

Figure 8 (6)(c), (d), and (e) - Alternative Table of Content Modifying Steps

Another style option you can use with the Table of Contents is font color. From the drop down list under **Font Color** select the color to use for your Table of Contents. But remember that too many font colors can make the Table of Contents hard to read.

In addition to formatting the Heading fonts, the line spacing should also be set-up. How much spacing you leave between each chapter heading in the `Table of Content is your choice. When choosing the line spacing, remember to consider your readers and how the spacing looks.

7. The Table of Contents can be single space, double space etc.

   a) Select the drop down arrow in the **Format** section and select **Paragraph** in the drop down field; confirm "Indents and Spacing" is selected;

   b) Confirm **Outline Level** matches the **TOC#** you are setting the line spacing for;

   c) Adjust the **Before**, **After**, **Line spacing** and **At** to the appropriate leading space (pt); and

   d) Review the line spacing in the **Preview** window to ensure the line spacing looks pleasing.

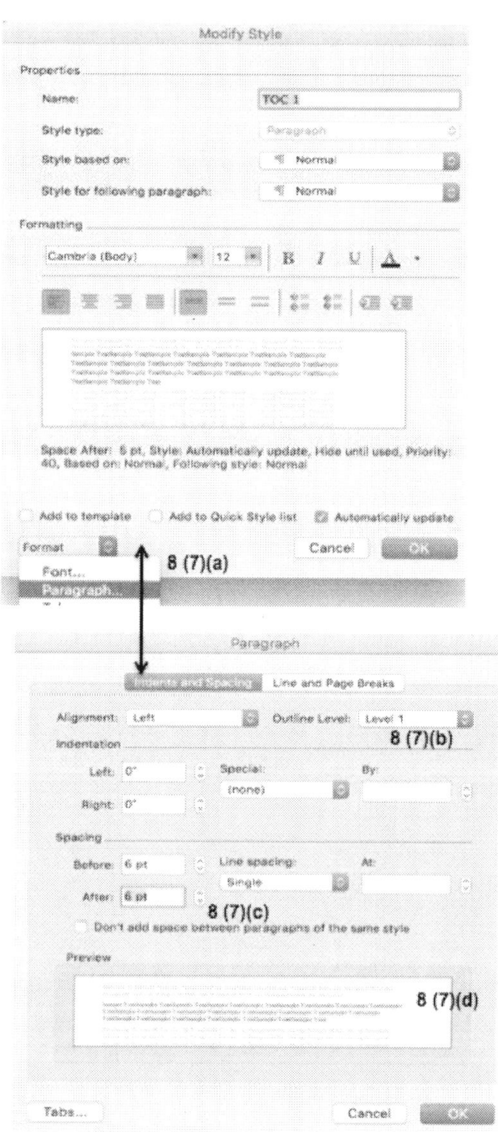

Figure 8 (7)(a) through (d) - Table of Content Paragraph Modify Steps

NOTE: If these square symbols appear in your document (with the ***Show/Hide*** *featured TURNED ON), it indicates that your paragraphs and sentences are formatted so the paragraphs and sentences are kept together. In your review of your document, if the paragraphs and sentences are marked with this format and do not look pleasing in your editorial review they can be removed by going to the* ***Paragraph*** *section and unchecking* ***Keep lines together*** *and* ***Keep with next*** *and then select* ***OK*** *to remove these squares.*

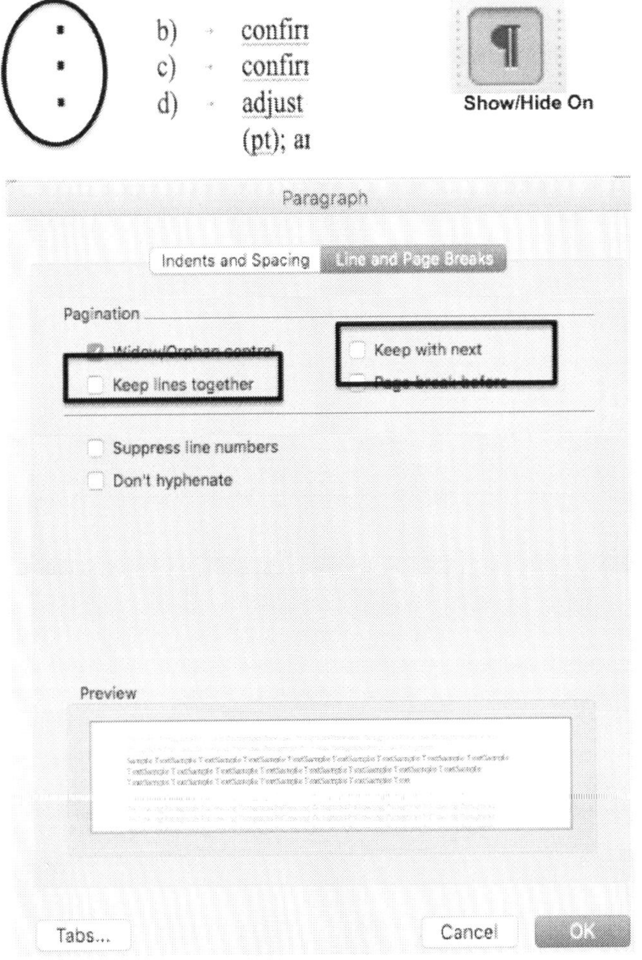

Example Square Symbols and Show/Hide Turned On and Paragraph Adjustment

8. Highlight the sub-chapter headings and select **Heading 2** from the tool bar.

CHAPTER 3A:	TERESA NEUERBURG
CHAPTER 4A:	JOSEPH
CHAPTER 4B:	EMMA
CHAPTER 4C:	WILLIAM
CHAPTER 4D:	VI
CHAPTER 4E:	CLARA
CHAPTER 4F:	WALT
CHAPTER 4G:	EDWARD

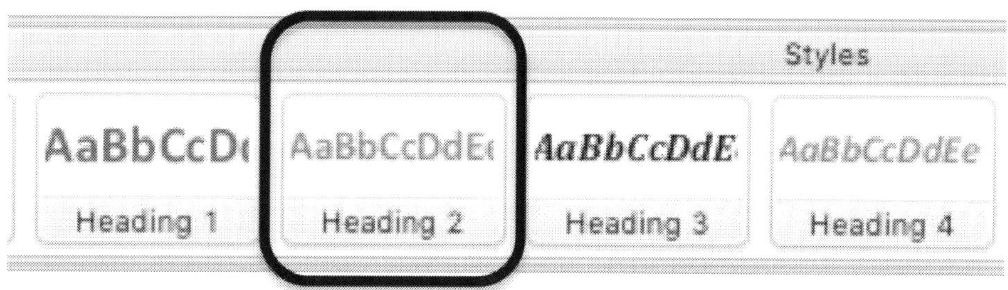

Figure 8 (8) - Sub-chapter Heading 2

9. Highlight sub-sub-chapter headings, and select **Heading 3**

CHAPTER 4C1:	HARRY
CHAPTER 4C2:	ROBERT
CHAPTER 4C3:	MARY LOU
CHAPTER 4D1:	DIXIE

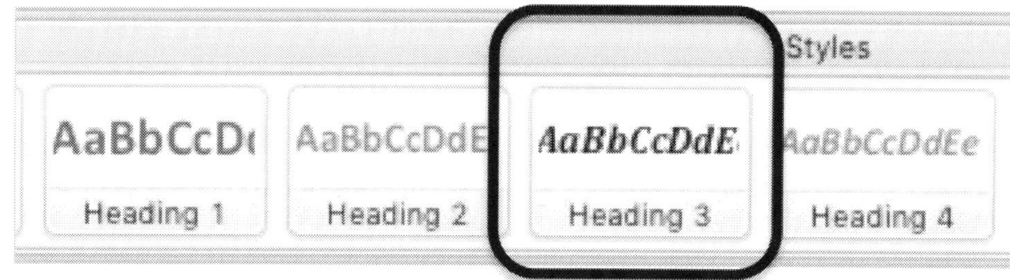

Figure 8 (9) - Sub-sub-chapter Heading 3

All chapter headings that are to be a part of your Table of Contents will need to have the format set for **Styles**, **Fonts**, and **Paragraph**. Steps 3 through 8 above should also be followed for sub-headings and sub-sub-headings.

Once the chapter headings and sub-headings are completed, it is time to insert your Table of Contents at the front of the book. The Table of Contents is usually on the page just before the first text page in the book.

Steps to Insert the Table of Contents

a) Place cursor on the page where the Table of Contents is to appear;

b) Select **Insert** from the Menu Bar and then select **Index and Tables**;

c) In the **Index and Tables** dialog, select **Table of Contents**;

d) Select the format (style) for the **Table of Contents**;

e) Select **Tab Leader**;

f) Review the **Preview** box to see if the **Leader** is to your liking; and

g) Select **OK** and the Table of Contents appears.

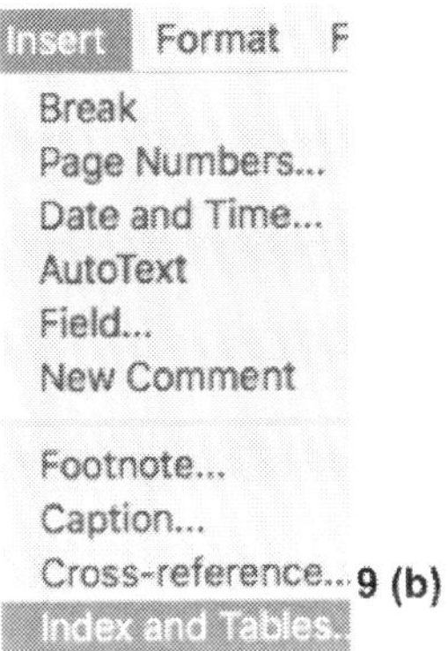

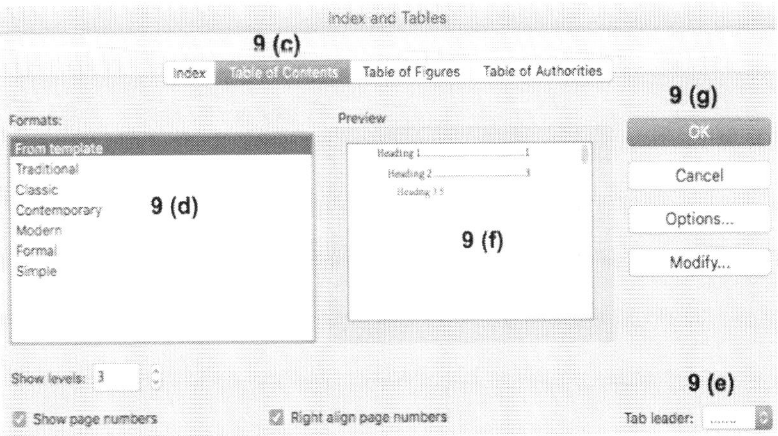

Figure 9 (a) through (g)- Steps to Insert Table of Contents

TABLE OF CONTENT

Example of Table of Contents

NOTE: If the chapter headings, sub-headings or sub-sub-headings are changed, the Table of Contents must be updated. The Table of Contents can be updated as follows:

a) Highlight the **Table of Contents**;

b) Select **Insert** from the Menu Bar and then select **Index and Tables**;

c) In the **Index and Tables** dialog, select **Table of Contents** and review the **Format**, **Tab Leader** and **Preview** boxes to verify your choices;

d) Select **OK**; and

e) When the dialog **Do you want to replace the selected Table of Contents?** appears, select **YES**.

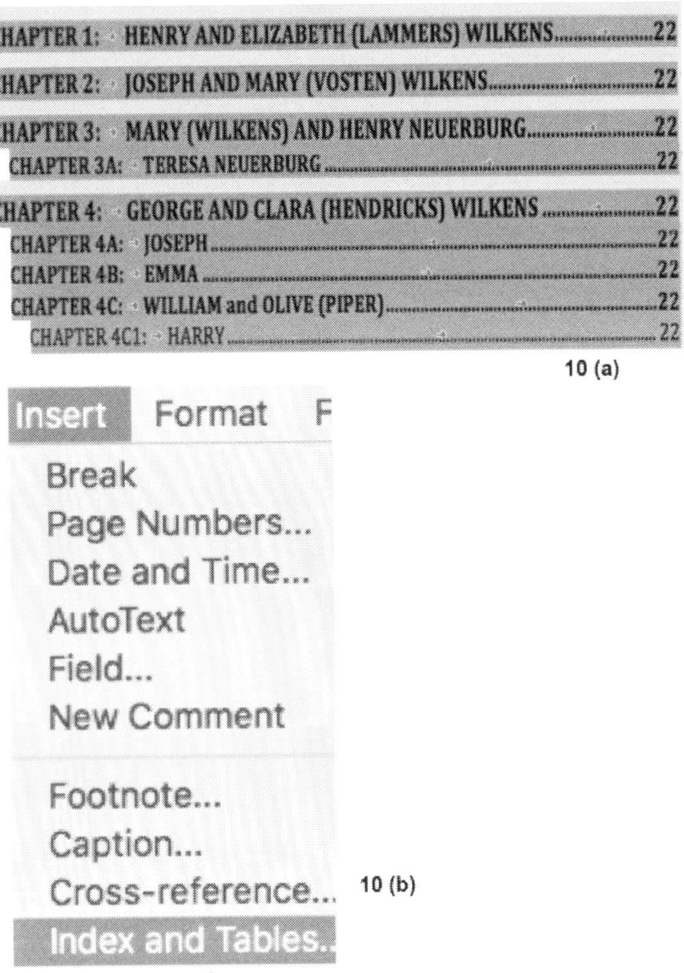

Figure 10 (a) through (e) - Table of Contents Updated

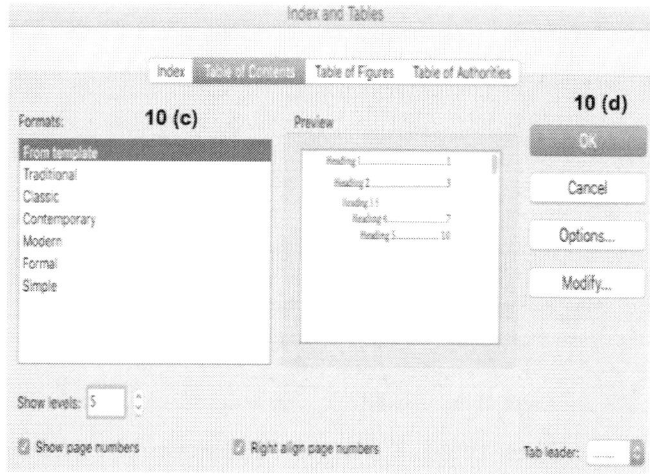

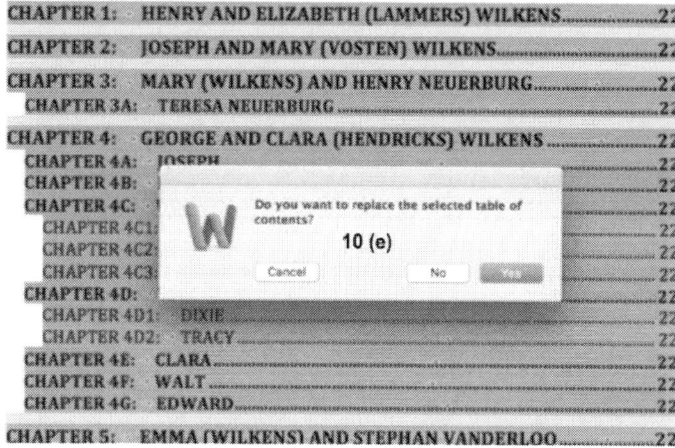

Figure 10 (c) through (e) - Table of Contents Updated

Another way to modify the Table of Content is by using the Styles tool bar.

a) Click on the **Heading #** to be modified in order to access the drop down field; and
b) Select **Modify** then follow steps 5 through 7 under the Table of Contents section.

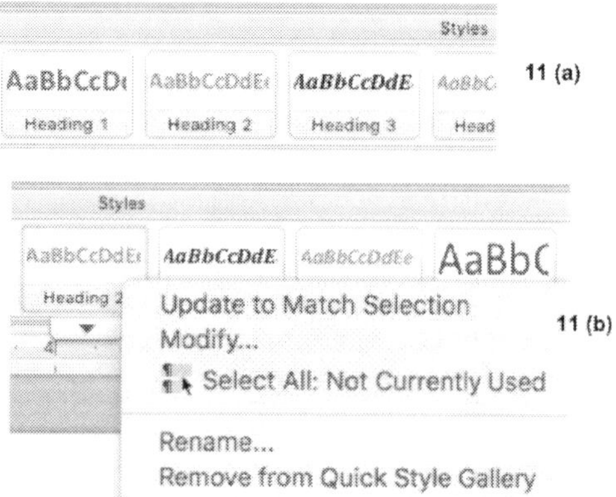

Figure 11 - Alternative Table of Contents Setup

Footnotes or Endnotes

The footnotes and endnotes are used for various purposes such as to provide bibliographical information, sources, copyright permission, explanatory information, citations or some additional details about the topic under consideration. The biggest difference between footnotes and endnotes is the placement of them in the book.

Footnotes are published at the bottom of the page while **Endnotes** are published at the end of the book.

Footnotes and endnotes can affect the length of the book. If a lot of footnotes are added to the bottom of the page there may not be much text on the page.

The pros and cons of footnotes and endnotes are:

Type	Pros	Cons
Footnotes	i. Gives an academic look and showcase for the research. ii. Instant access at bottom of page to the research citations, supplemental thoughts, ideas or concepts. iii. Footnotes are considered outdated, but some institutions and professional fields still require footnotes to be used.	i. Interrupts the flow by drawing the eyes away from the text. ii. A lot of footnotes on a single page can make the page appear cluttered or difficult to read. iii. If footnotes are lengthy, the footnotes may dominate the page and distract from the page.
Endnotes	i. Less distracting to the reader. ii. Does not clutter the page. iii. Provides the research list in one place. iv. Allows the reader to look over and digest the research information as a whole as the research is in one place. v. Can be placed at the end of a chapter or at the end of the book.	i. Readers must go to the end of the book to review the research information. ii. Readers might see endnotes as misleading or that the author is trying to hide the research. iii. Placement can make it difficult to find the endnotes.
In-text citations	Doesn't distract readers since sources are integrated within the text.	Adds extra words and can sound clumsy or forced.

Table 5 - Footnotes and Endnotes

As you can see from Table 5, footnotes and endnotes do have a few things in common.

- The reference numbers for a footnote or endnote are placed at the end of the sentence, phrase or quotation because this minimizes the interruption in the flow of words.
- Both are noted with consecutive, superscript numerals.
- The referenced numbers found in the text will have the same matching number appearing at the beginning of the actual footnote or endnote.

Using footnotes, endnotes, or in-text citations will depend on whether you are writing for a journal, newspaper, magazine, college, etc. and whether these institutions have specific guidelines that must be followed.

If no guidelines are required, the writer may use footnotes, endnotes, or in-text citations.

Tips When Using Footnotes and Endnotes

- Place footnote or endnote numbers at the end of sentences.
- Use care in formatting so they are formatted properly.
- The tab or indent for a footnote and endnote should be a minimum of 5 spaces from the left margin. The second and subsequent lines of a Footnote or Endnote should not be indented.
- Leave one space between the superscript number and the entry.
- Consecutively number footnotes and endnotes using a superscript, e.g.,1.
- Some paragraphs call for more than one footnote or endnote, which brings to question, does the reference number of the footnote or endnote go at the end of the paragraph or end of each sentence? Either can be used, but it is important to be consistent.
- Formatting footnotes and endnotes depends on the official institution's guidelines you are required to follow.
- Overusing footnotes or endnotes can hurt the strength of the book and/or paper.
- The superscript number used in the text should be the same superscript number used for the footnote and/or endnote.
- Endnotes should start on a new page at the end of the book and be before the Bibliography.

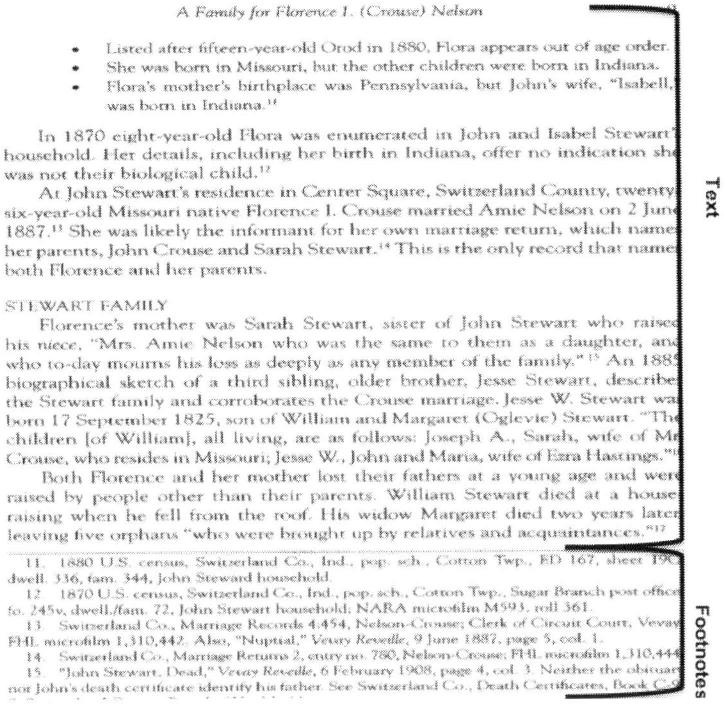

A Family for Florence I. (Crouse) Nelson

- Listed after fifteen-year-old Orod in 1880, Flora appears out of age order.
- She was born in Missouri, but the other children were born in Indiana.
- Flora's mother's birthplace was Pennsylvania, but John's wife, "Isabell," was born in Indiana.[11]

In 1870 eight-year-old Flora was enumerated in John and Isabel Stewart's household. Her details, including her birth in Indiana, offer no indication she was not their biological child.[12]

At John Stewart's residence in Center Square, Switzerland County, twenty-six-year-old Missouri native Florence I. Crouse married Amie Nelson on 2 June 1887.[13] She was likely the informant for her own marriage return, which names her parents, John Crouse and Sarah Stewart.[14] This is the only record that names both Florence and her parents.

STEWART FAMILY

Florence's mother was Sarah Stewart, sister of John Stewart who raised his niece, "Mrs. Amie Nelson who was the same to them as a daughter, and who to-day mourns his loss as deeply as any member of the family."[15] An 188[illegible] biographical sketch of a third sibling, older brother, Jesse Stewart, describes the Stewart family and corroborates the Crouse marriage. Jesse W. Stewart was born 17 September 1825, son of William and Margaret (Oglevie) Stewart. "The children [of William], all living, are as follows: Joseph A., Sarah, wife of Mr. Crouse, who resides in Missouri; Jesse W., John and Maria, wife of Ezra Hastings."[1[illegible]]

Both Florence and her mother lost their fathers at a young age and were raised by people other than their parents. William Stewart died at a house raising when he fell from the roof. His widow Margaret died two years later leaving five orphans "who were brought up by relatives and acquaintances."[17]

Text

11. 1880 U.S. census, Switzerland Co., Ind., pop. sch., Cotton Twp., ED 167, sheet 19C, dwell. 336, fam. 344, John Steward household.

12. 1870 U.S. census, Switzerland Co., Ind., pop. sch., Cotton Twp., Sugar Branch post office, fo. 245v, dwell./fam. 72, John Stewart household; NARA microfilm M593, roll 361.

13. Switzerland Co., Marriage Records 4:454, Nelson-Crouse; Clerk of Circuit Court, Vevay; FHL microfilm 1,310,442. Also, "Nuptial," *Vevay Reveille*, 9 June 1887, page 5, col. 1.

14. Switzerland Co., Marriage Returns 2, entry no. 780, Nelson-Crouse; FHL microfilm 1,310,44[illegible]

15. "John Stewart, Dead," *Vevay Reveille*, 6 February 1908, page 4, col. 3. Neither the obituary nor John's death certificate identify his father. See Switzerland Co., Death Certificates, Book C-[illegible]

Footnotes

Figure 12 - Footnote Example

ENDNOTES

[1] Hussein, Radiyyah, "What is a Realist? How to Tell if You Have a Realist Personality." Article. *CogniFit Health, Brain & Neuroscience*. https://blog.cognifit.com/what-is-a -realist-8-signs-to-tell-if-you-have-a-realist-personality/ ; posted 29 March 2018.

[2] Wikimedia Foundation, Inc., "Life Expectancy." Website. *Wikipedia The Free Encyclopedia*. https://en.wikipedia.org/wiki/Life_expectancy : posted 3 September 2018.

[3] Wikimedia Foundation, Inc., "To Tell the Truth." Website. *Wikipedia The Free Encyclopedia*. https://en.wikipedia.org/wiki/To_Tell_the_Truth : posted 5 September 2018.

[4] Lafreniere, Luke, "What are Fonts and Typefaces?" YouTube. *Techquickie*. https://www.youtube.com/watch?v=l2iNthl-RUk : posted 27 May 2016.

[5] United States Patent and Trademark Office (USPTO), "General information concerning patents." Website. *Inventor Resources*. https://www.uspto.gov/patents-getting-started/general-information-concerning-patents : posted 14 March 2018.

Figure 13 - Endnote Example

Inserting Footnotes and Endnotes

Place the cursor at the end of the sentence:

a) Select **Insert** from the Menu Bar and then select **Footnote**;
b) After the **Footnote and Endnote** dialog appears select either **Footnotes** or **Endnotes**;
c) Select **Number format** or **Custom mark**;
d) Select **Start** at;
e) Select **Numbering**;
f) Select **Apply changes to**;
g) Select **Insert**; and
h) Then select **Apply**

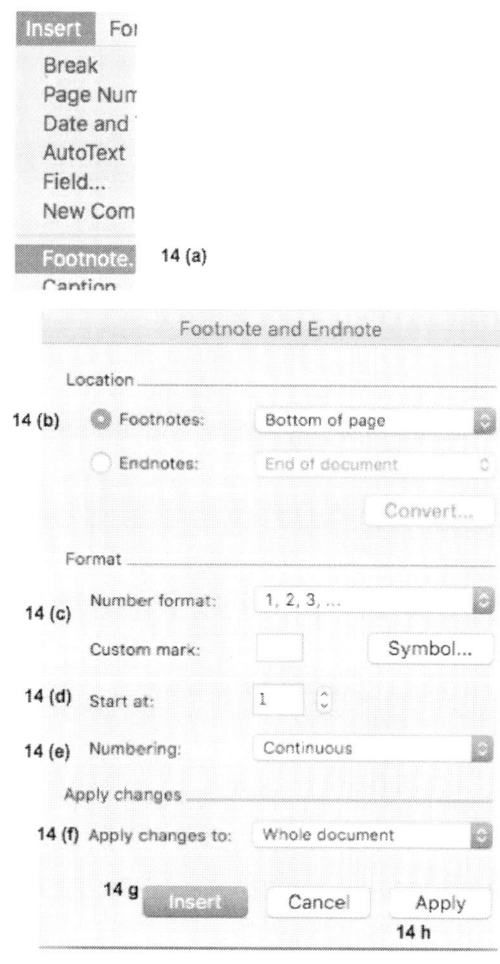

Figure 14 (a) through 14 (h) - Steps to Setup Footnotes and Endnotes

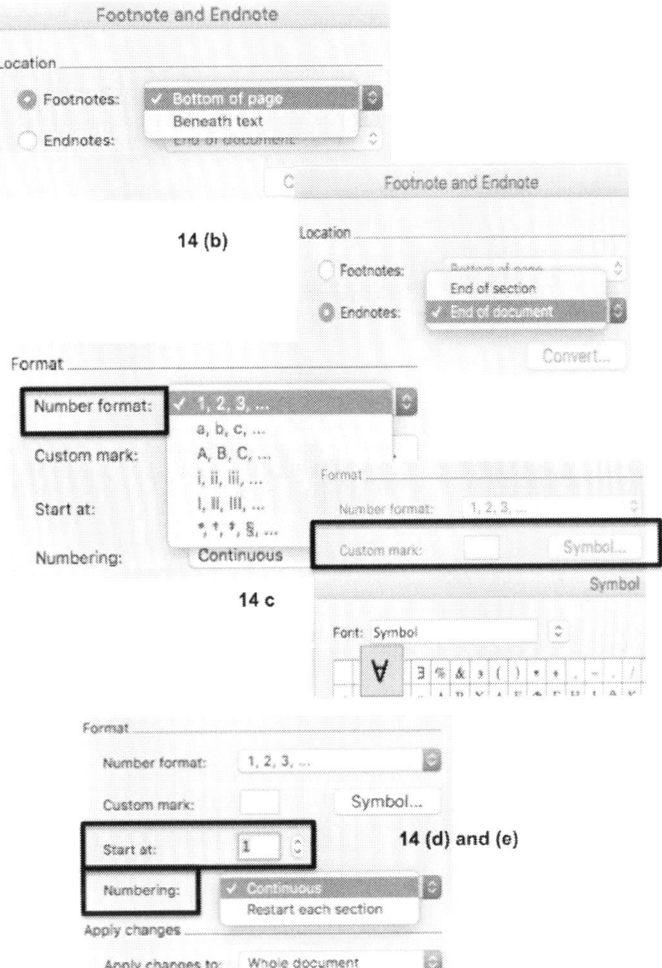

Tables of Figures and Charts

If you decide to include tables, figures or photographs, you may wish to include a list of them in the book. Much like a Table of Contents page, a Table of Figures page can help your readers find the relevant information easier and quicker.

The Table of Figures page is usually at the start of the document and is just after the Table of Contents. If you are using several different charts, figures, tables, you may want to use a separate list for all of the charts, figures, and tables referenced in the book.

Inserting Figures and Charts Captions

a) Right click on the image figure, table or chart.
   [*Note: a blue box with dots will appear around the figure, table or chart.*];

b) Select **Insert** from the Menu Bar and then select **Caption**;

c) The **Caption** dialog will appear;

d) Complete the **Caption** fields for the figure, table, or chart;

e) Click on the **Label** drop down field in the **Option** section and select the appropriate label for your figure, equation, table;

f) Click on the **Position** drop down field in the **Option** section and select either **Above selected item** or **Below selected item**;

g) Select **Numbering** and choose the number styling you wish to use;

h) Then click **OK**.

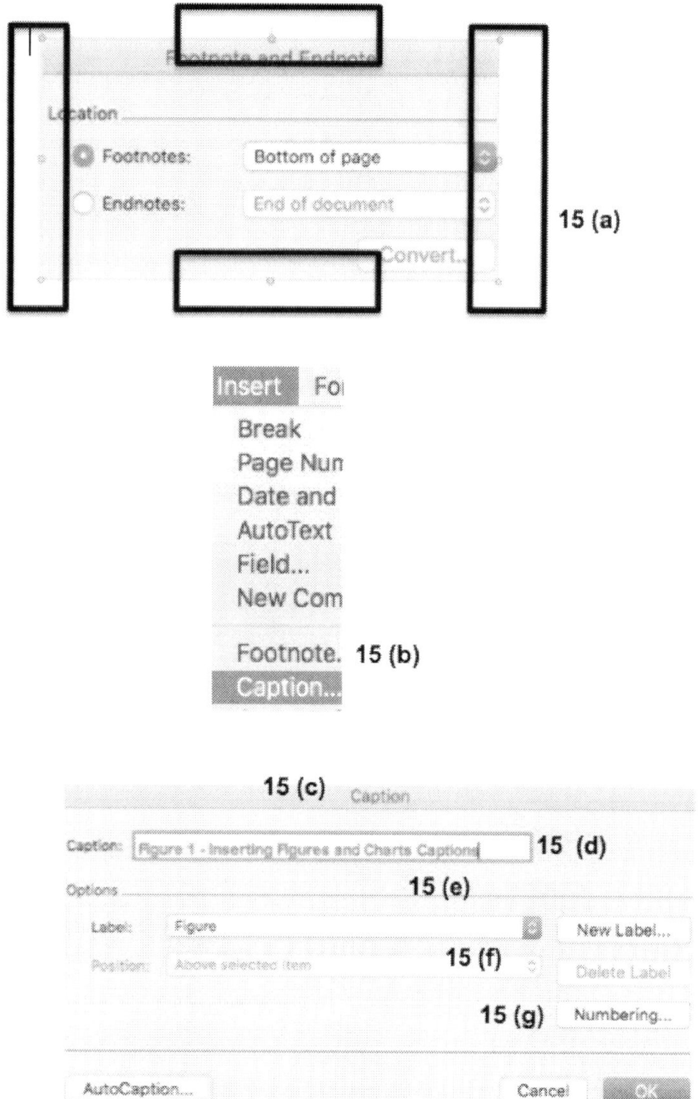

Figure 15 - Steps (a) through (h) to add Captions to Figures, Tables, and Charts

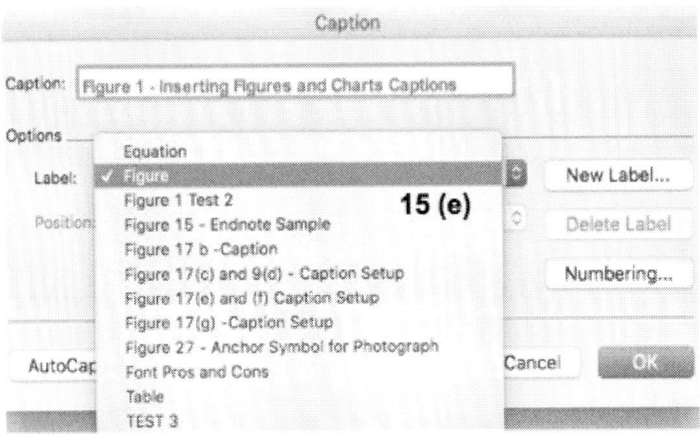
Caption
Caption: Figure 1 - Inserting Figures and Charts Captions
Options
Equation
Label:
Figure
Figure 1 Test 2
15 (e)
Position
Figure 15 - Endnote Sample
Figure 17 b -Caption
Figure 17(c) and 9(d) - Caption Setup
Figure 17(e) and (f) Caption Setup
Figure 17(g) -Caption Setup
Figure 27 - Anchor Symbol for Photograph
Font Pros and Cons
Table
TEST 3
New Label...
Delete Label
Numbering...
Cancel
OK

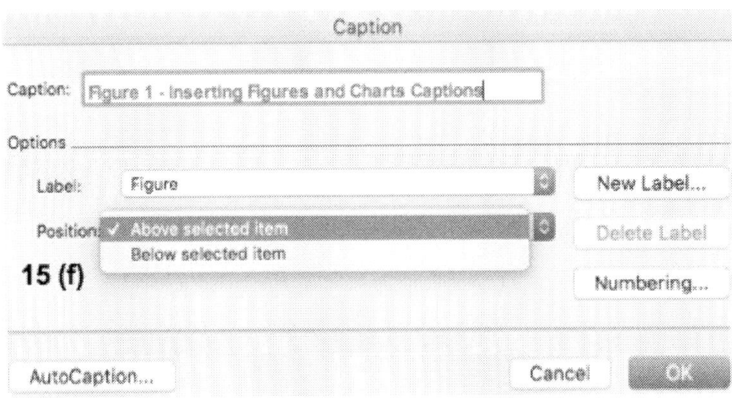
Caption
Caption: Figure 1 - Inserting Figures and Charts Captions
Options
Label: Figure
Position: Above selected item
Below selected item
15 (f)
New Label...
Delete Label
Numbering...
AutoCaption...
Cancel
OK

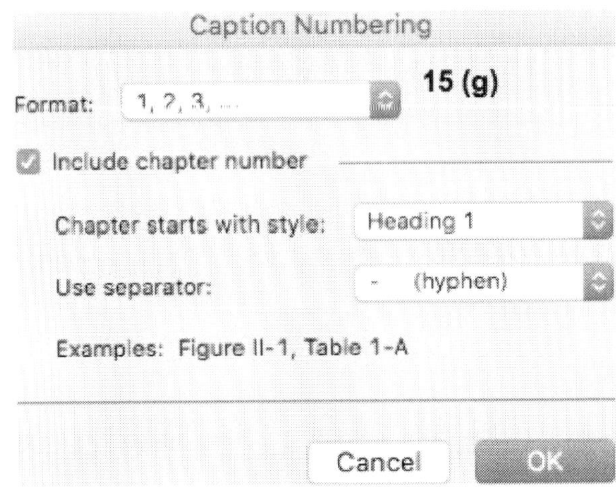
Caption Numbering
Format: 1, 2, 3, ...
15 (g)
Include chapter number
Chapter starts with style: Heading 1
Use separator: - (hyphen)
Examples: Figure II-1, Table 1-A
Cancel
OK

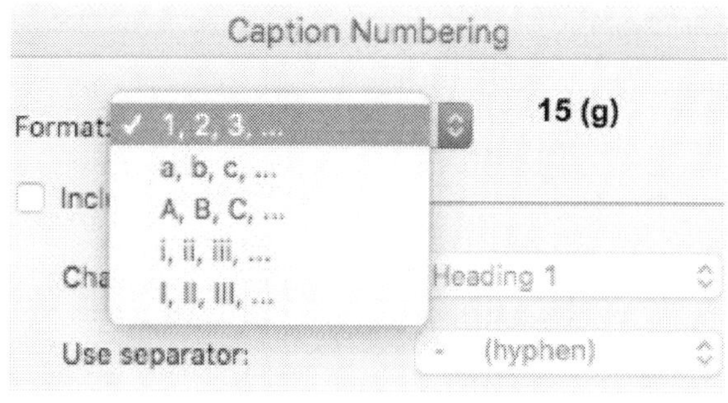

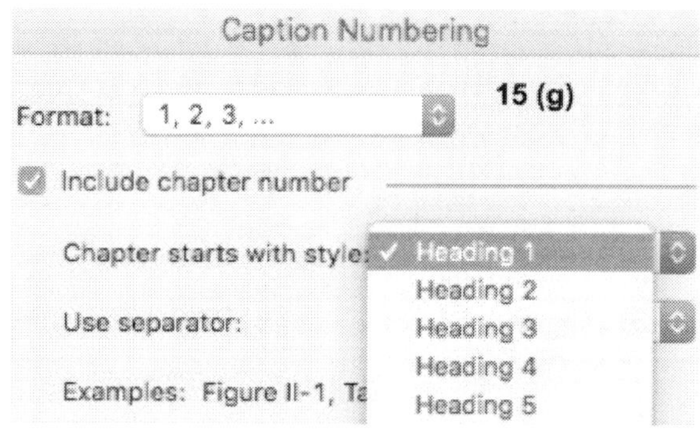

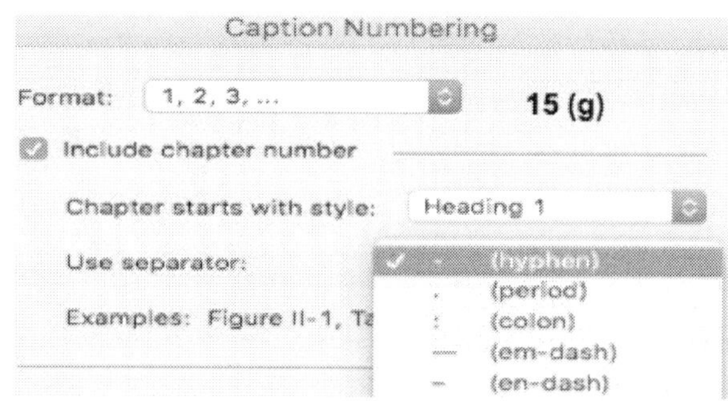

Insert Table of Figures and Charts Pages

a) Place cursor on the page you want the **Table of Figures** to appear;
b) Select **Insert** from the Menu Bar and then select **Index and Tables**;
c) The **Index and Tables** dialog opens, select **Table of Figures**;
d) Select the **Caption Label** for the type of table you are setting up, i.e., Figure or Table;
e) Select the **Format** style for the **Table of Figures**;
f) Select **Tab Leader**;
g) Review the **Preview** box to see if the Leader is to your liking; and
h) Select **OK** and the Table of Figures will appear where you have placed the cursor.

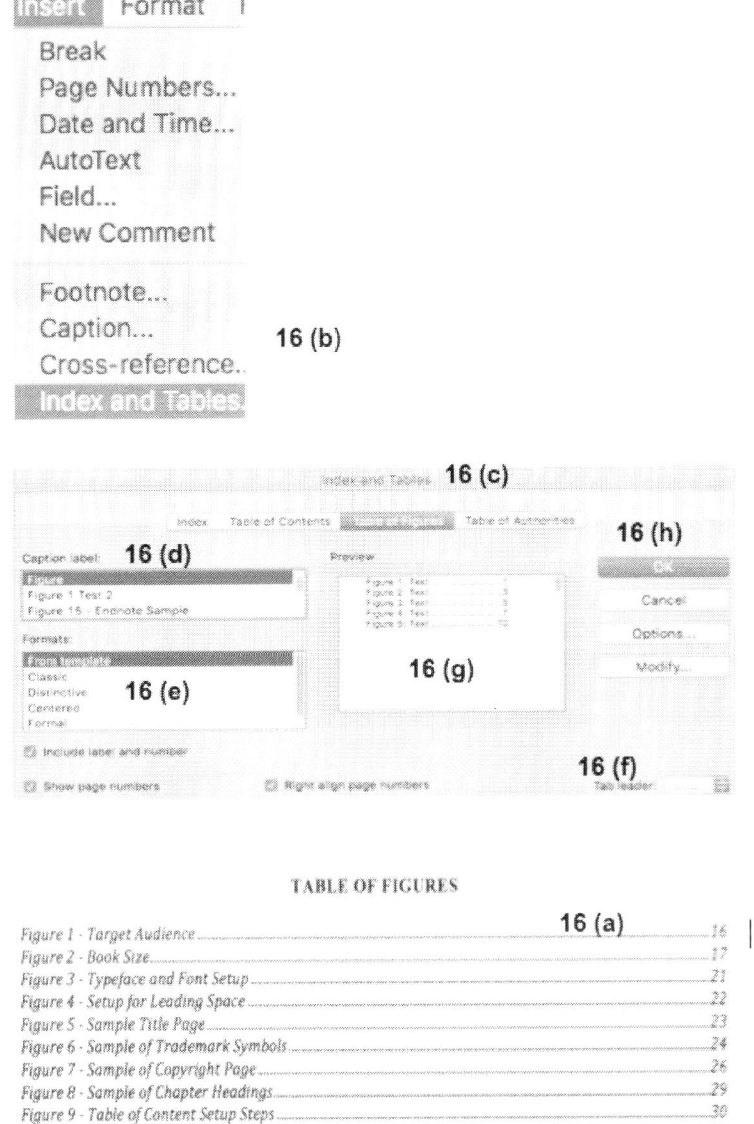

Figure 16 - Steps (a) through (h) to Insert Table of Figures and Charts Page

NOTE: If the figures, tables or charts captions are changed, the Table of Figures will need to be updated as follows:

a) Highlight the table of figures;
b) Select **Insert** from the Menu Bar and then select **Index and Tables** (see Figure 16(b));
c) In the **Index and Tables** dialog select **Table of Figures** (see Figure 16(c));
d) Review the **Preview** box to see if the **Caption Label**, **Formats** and **Tab Leader** is to your liking (see Figure 16(d), 16(e), 16(f) and 16(g));
e) Select **OK**; the dialog **Do you want to replace the selected Table of Contents?** appears, then select **YES**.

TABLE OF FIGURES 17 (a)

TABLE OF FIGURES

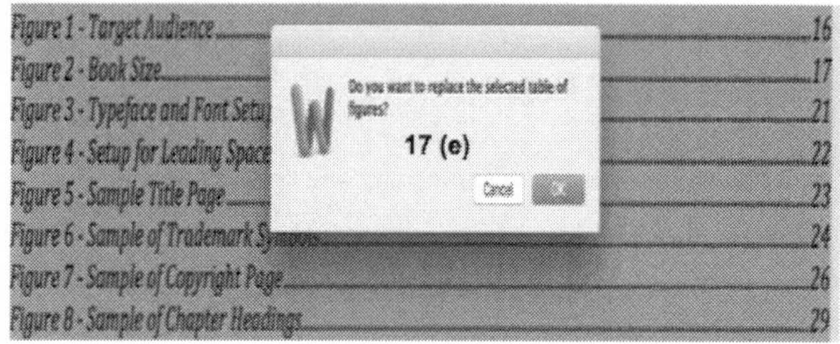

Figure 17 (a) and (e) - Example of Table of Figures Modified and Updated

Using Page Numbers

Adding page numbers to your book makes it easier for the reader to find information. In addition, readers are familiar with page numbers and if the page numbers are omitted it could cause confusion for readers as well as librarians, printers and archivists. Page numbers are essential for many people who interact with books. For example, page numbers help printers to determine if a page was missed during the printing process.

The benefit of page numbers allows you to (i) determine if there is a page missing; (ii) determine if the pages are in the correct order; and (iii) reference specific pages.

A few guidelines you may want to follow when using page names:

- Use Roman numerals for the front matter;
- Isolate blank pages in their own sections (remove **Same as Previous**);
- Use an **Odd Page Break** at the end of the front matter, and before all elements that have to begin on a right hand page;
- Use Arabic numerals for the main body text and back matter; and
- Put page numbers in your footers to avoid losing page numbers.

Page Number Styles

Page	Numbering
Blank (or title)	i
Frontispiece (or blank)	ii
Title page	iii
Copyright	iv
Dedication	v
Blank	vi
Table of Contents	vii
List of Illustration	odd
Foreword	odd

Table 6 - Example of Page Numbering Styles

Before spending time adding page numbers to your book, I would recommend reaching out to your publisher for advice on the best format for your page numbers. Page numbers can be located on the top or bottom of a page and can be centered, flush right or flush left. When a page number is located at the bottom of the page, you may hear your publisher or editor refer to these page numbers as *drop folios*.

Another benefit to using page numbers is the assistance it gives in setting up an index for the book. An index is a wonderful addition to a book, since it can help the reader locate the exact page for a specific term or concept.

When I prepared my family genealogy book, I used page numbers so the names mentioned throughout my book would be included in the index page with the corresponding page number. Including the index with the appropriate page numbers allowed family members to search and find their ancestor much easier.

Preparing the Index

An Index in a book is a wonderful tool for locating the important material in the book. The Index can be set up with various degrees of importance by categorizing entries as **Main Entries** and **Subentries**.

A **Main Entry** represents the highest level in the index while a **Subentry** represents the next lower level in the index. For example, the Subentry may be the children of the person marked in the Main Entry. To distinguish between the Main Entry and Subentry levels in the Index, you may wish the Main Entry to be in bold formatting.

Cross-referencing is used when the text is to be found on additional pages in the book. For example if a daughter marries, the daughter's maiden name is given along with the daughter's married name. In order to create an Index, the content material to be included in the Index must be marked.

Steps to Set Up Mark Entry Codes:

a) Select **Insert** from the **Tool Bar** and then **Index and Tables**;

b) After the **Index and Tables** dialog opens select **Index**;

c) Select the format style for the Index and review the **Preview** box to see if the Index style is acceptable;

d) Place cursor on or at the end of the word to be marked for the Index;
NOTE: To see the Mark Entry codes in the text of the book, the special characters, which Word refers to as nonprinting characters or show/hide, must be turned on (see *Figure 19 (a) and (b)).*

e) Click on **Mark Entry**;

f) The **Mark Index Entry** dialog appears;

g) In the **Mark Entry** dialog complete the following boxes. *NOTE: this sample index represents an index for a family genealogy book; if it is not an index for a family genealogy book the word you wish to index will need to be used in the boxes.*

Henry was born in Germany in 1840 and married Elizabeth Lammers .... Elizabeth is the daughter of Gerhard and Anna (Wuebben) Lammers ... John Henry and

18 (d)

Figure 18 (a) through (g) - Steps to Set Up Mark Entry Codes

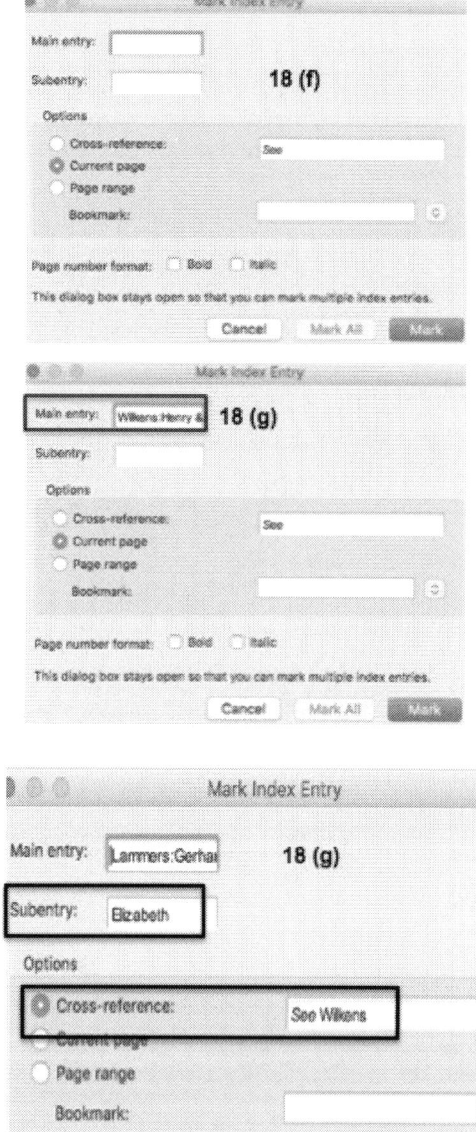

Figure 18 (f) through (g)

Main Entry Setup

a) Enter the surname in the **Main Entry** dialog;
   Be sure to use a semicolon [:] after the surname;

b) Select **Current Page**;

c) Select **Bold** in the **Page number format** section; and

d) Select **Mark** and the marked entry will show up in the body of the text as follows

{ XE "**Wilkens**:Henry & Elizabeth (Lammers)" }

Subentry Setup

a) Enter the surname marked in the **Main Entry** dialog
Be sure to use a semicolon [:] after the surname in the **Main Entry** box;

b) Enter the first name of the person in the **Subentry** box;

c) Select the **Current Page**; and

d) Select **Mark** and the marked entry will show up in the body of the text as follows

{ XE "**Wilkens**:Henry & Elizabeth (Lammers):Joseph Henry" }

Cross-reference Setup

a) Enter the surname marked in the **Main Entry** box
Be sure to use a semicolon [:] after the surname in the **Main Entry** box;

b) Enter the first name of the person in the **Subentr**y box;

c) Click the **Cross-reference**

d) After the word "see" enter the new surname for the person. For example, if the daughter's maiden name is Smith there will be a Subentry for the daughter under the Main entry for Smith. And if the daughter married a man named Jones the daughter will now show under the Main entry for Jones.

e) Select **Current Page**; and

f) Select **Mark** and the marked entry will show up in the body of the text as follows

{ XE "**Lammers**:Gerhard & Anna (Wuebben):Elizabeth" \t "*See* Wilkens" }

NOTE: To turn the invisible characters on and off click on the Show/Hide Button:

Figure 19 (a)

Show/Hide Button 'on'
when grayed out

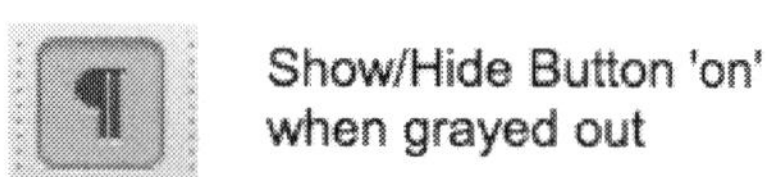

{ XE "**Lammers**:Gerhard & Anna (Wuebben):Elizabeth" \t "See Wilkens" }

Example of Show/Hide Button 'on' to show
Mark Entry Codes 'on'

Figure 19 (b)

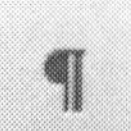

Show/Hide Button 'off'
when not grayed out

Henry was born in Germany in 1840 and married Elizabeth … Elizabeth is the daughter of Gerhard and Anna (Wuebben) Lammers. Henry

Example of Show/Hide Button 'off' to show Mark Entry
Codes 'off'

Figure 19 (a) and (b) - Example Show/Hide Button in the "On" and "Off" Position Showing Mark Entry Codes on and off

Tips When Preparing the Mark Entry Code

If you elect to style your Index with bold formatting and/or highlight words, the first time you setup the Mark Entry code, which contains the word to be bold and/or highlighted will need to be bold and highlighted in the first Mark Entry code. Only the very first code of the Mark Entry needs to be bold and/or highlighted.

Henry was born in Germany in 1840 and married Elizabeth Lammers { XE "**Wilkens**:Henry & Elizabeth (Lammers)" }on January 17, 1871 ... Elizabeth is the daughter of Gerhard and Anna (Wuebben) Lammers. { XE "**Lammers**:Gerhard & Anna (Wuebben):Elizabeth" \t "*See* Wilkens" } ... children are: ¶

¶

Joseph Henry { XE "Wilkens:Henry & Elizabeth (Lammers):Joseph Henry & Mary" }was born ... Mary (Wulkotte) Vorsten on ... Mary is the daughter of Gerhard and Gertrude (Kuepert) Wulkotte. { XE "**Wulkotte**:Gerhard & Gertrude (Keupert):Mary" \t "*See* Vorsten & Wilkens" } Mary's first marriage was to Albert Vorsten { XE "**Vorsten**:Albert & Mary" }on January .... ¶

INDEX

Figure 20 - Example of Bold and Highlighted Mark Entry Codes and Index

NOTE: If you wish your index to include other styles or characters, i.e., italic, underline, or special characters (@, #, $), these styles and special characters will also need to be inserted in the first Mark Entry code of the text.

Inserting the Index and Modifying the Index

Once all surnames (or words) have been marked for the index, the next step is to create the index at the end of the book.

a) The Show/Hide toggle button must be turned OFF;
NOTE: It is important to turn off the Show/Hide feature so the page numbers will be accurate in the Index;

b) Place cursor on the page where the index is to be inserted;

c) Select **Insert** on the Menu Bar and then select **Index and Tables** (see Figure 18(a));

d) In the **Index and Tables** dialog, select **Index**;

e) Select either **Indented** or **Run-in** in the **Type** section;

f) Select the format for the Index in the **Formats** section;

g) Select the **Number of Columns** for the Index;
NOTE: be careful on how many columns you select because too many columns will make the Index hard to read and appear crowded.

h) Check either the box for **Headings for Accented Letters** or **Right Align Page Numbers**;

i) Select a **Tab Leader** style;

j) Review your selections in the **Preview** section;

k) Select **OK**; and

l) The Index will appear on the page where the cursor was placed.

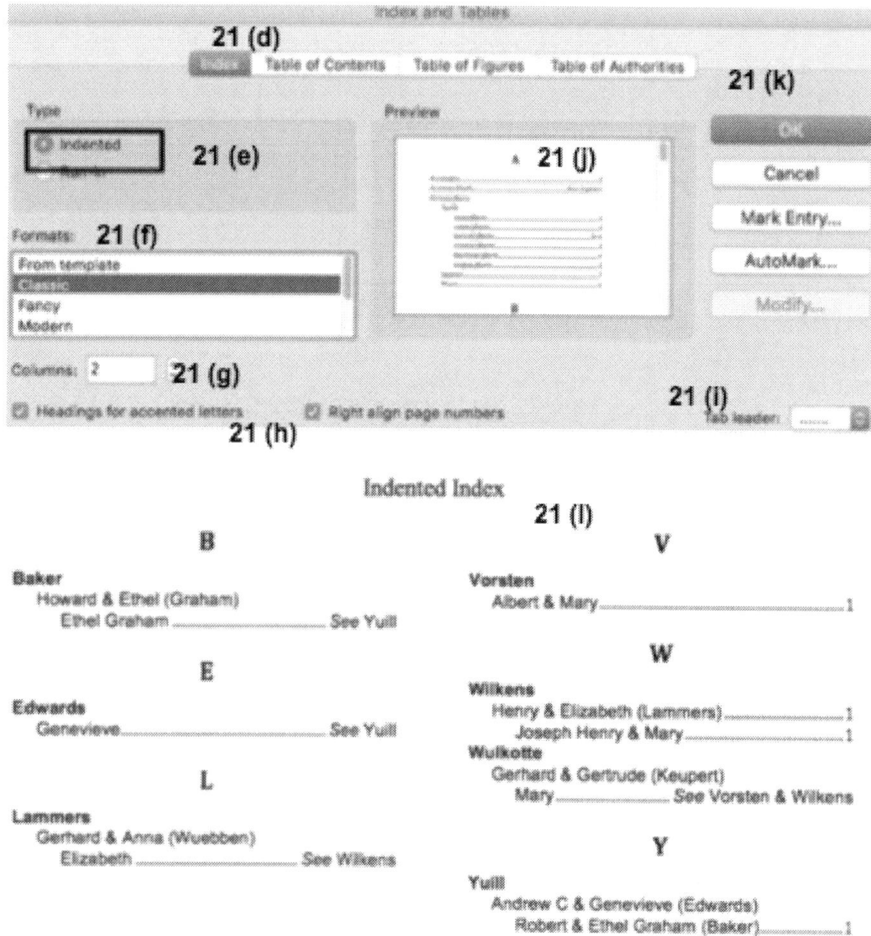

Figure 21 (d) through (l) - Inserting Index Steps

Run-in Setup and Index

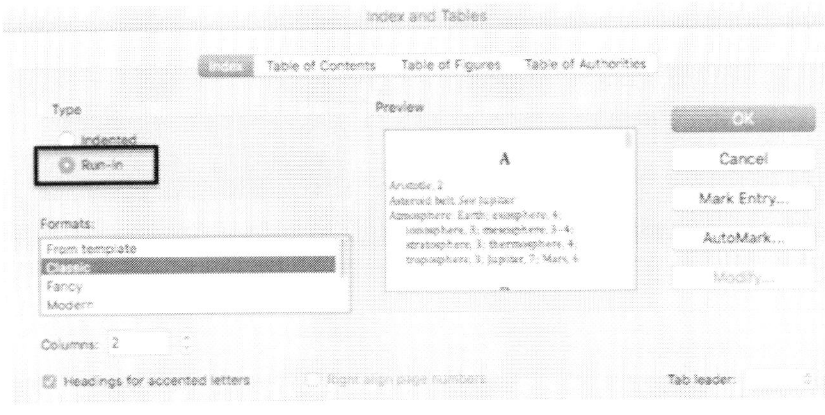

Run-in Index

B

Baker: Howard & Ethel (Graham); Ethel Graham. *See* Yuill

E

Edwards: Genevieve. *See* Yuill

L

Lammers: Gerhard & Anna (Wuebben); Elizabeth. *See* Wilkens

V

Vorsten: Albert & Mary, 1

W

Wilkens: Henry & Elizabeth (Lammers), 1; Joseph Henry & Mary, 1

Wulkotte: Gerhard & Gertrude (Keupert); Mary. *See* Vorsten & Wilkens

Y

Yuill: Andrew C & Genevieve (Edwards); Robert & Ethel Graham (Baker), 1

NOTE: If any names are added or revised after the initial text draft and index setup, a Mark Entry code will need to be completed for the new names. Once a Mark Entry code has been completed for the new names, the Index will need to be updated.

Steps to Setup Modified Index with New Names

a) Update the text with the new names to be added to the Index;

b) Enter the **Mark Entry** codes for the new names by following either the (a) **Main Entry Setup** steps; (b) **Subentry Setup** steps; or (c) **Cross-reference Setup** steps.

c) Highlight the Index;

d) Select **Insert** on the Menu Bar and then select **Index Tables**;

e) In the **Index and Tables** dialog and select **Index**;

f) Select either **Indented** or **Run-in** in the **Type** section;

g) Select the format for the Index in the **Formats** section;

h) Verify the **number of Columns** for the Index;

i) Check either the box for **Headings for Accented Letters** or **Right Align Page Numbers**;

j) Select a **Tab Leader** style;

k) Review your selections in the **Preview** section;

l) Select **OK**; and

m) In the **Do you want to replace the selected Index?** dialog, select **YES**;

n) The modified Index will be updated with the new names;

Marked Entry Codes for New Names

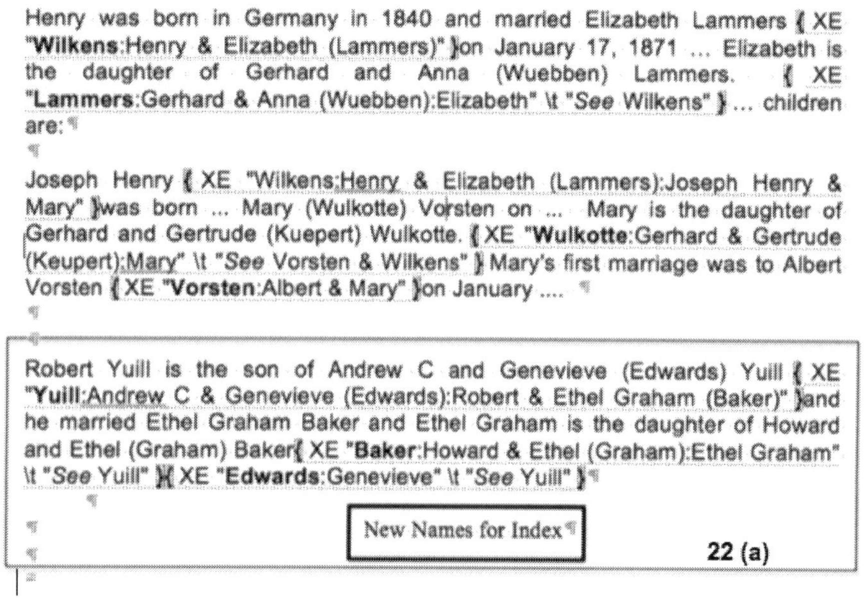

Henry was born in Germany in 1840 and married Elizabeth Lammers { XE "**Wilkens**:Henry & Elizabeth (Lammers)" }on January 17, 1871 ... Elizabeth is the daughter of Gerhard and Anna (Wuebben) Lammers. { XE "**Lammers**:Gerhard & Anna (Wuebben):Elizabeth" \t "*See* Wilkens" } ... children are:

Joseph Henry { XE "Wilkens:Henry & Elizabeth (Lammers):Joseph Henry & Mary" }was born ... Mary (Wulkotte) Vorsten on ... Mary is the daughter of Gerhard and Gertrude (Kuepert) Wulkotte. { XE "**Wulkotte**:Gerhard & Gertrude (Keupert):Mary" \t "*See* Vorsten & Wilkens" } Mary's first marriage was to Albert Vorsten { XE "**Vorsten**:Albert & Mary" }on January ....

Robert Yuill is the son of Andrew C and Genevieve (Edwards) Yuill { XE "**Yuill**:Andrew C & Genevieve (Edwards):Robert & Ethel Graham (Baker)" }and he married Ethel Graham Baker and Ethel Graham is the daughter of Howard and Ethel (Graham) Baker{ XE "**Baker**:Howard & Ethel (Graham):Ethel Graham" \t "*See* Yuill" }{ XE "**Edwards**:Genevieve" \t "*See* Yuill" }

New Names for Index

22 (a)

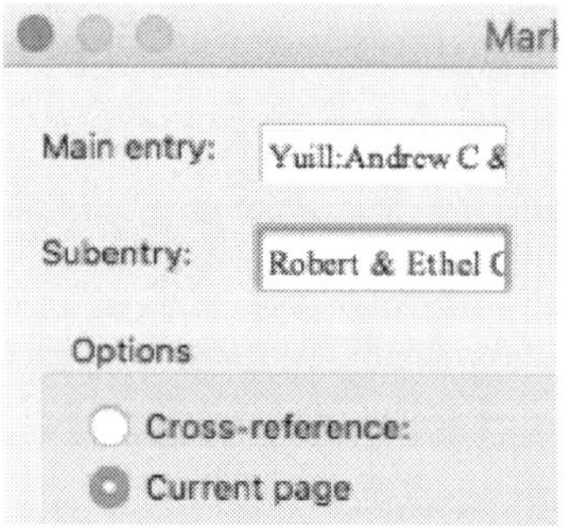

Mark

Main entry: Yuill:Andrew C &

Subentry: Robert & Ethel G

Options

Cross-reference:

Current page

22 (b)

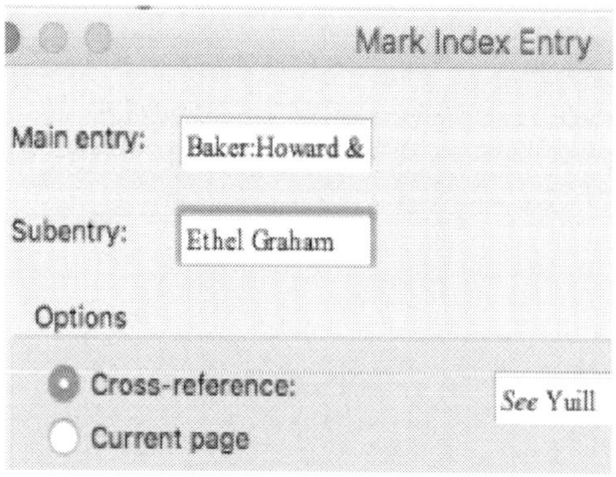

Mark Index Entry

Main entry: Baker:Howard &

Subentry: Ethel Graham

Options

Cross-reference: *See* Yuill

Current page

Figure 22 (a) through (n) - Example of Marked Entry Codes for New Names

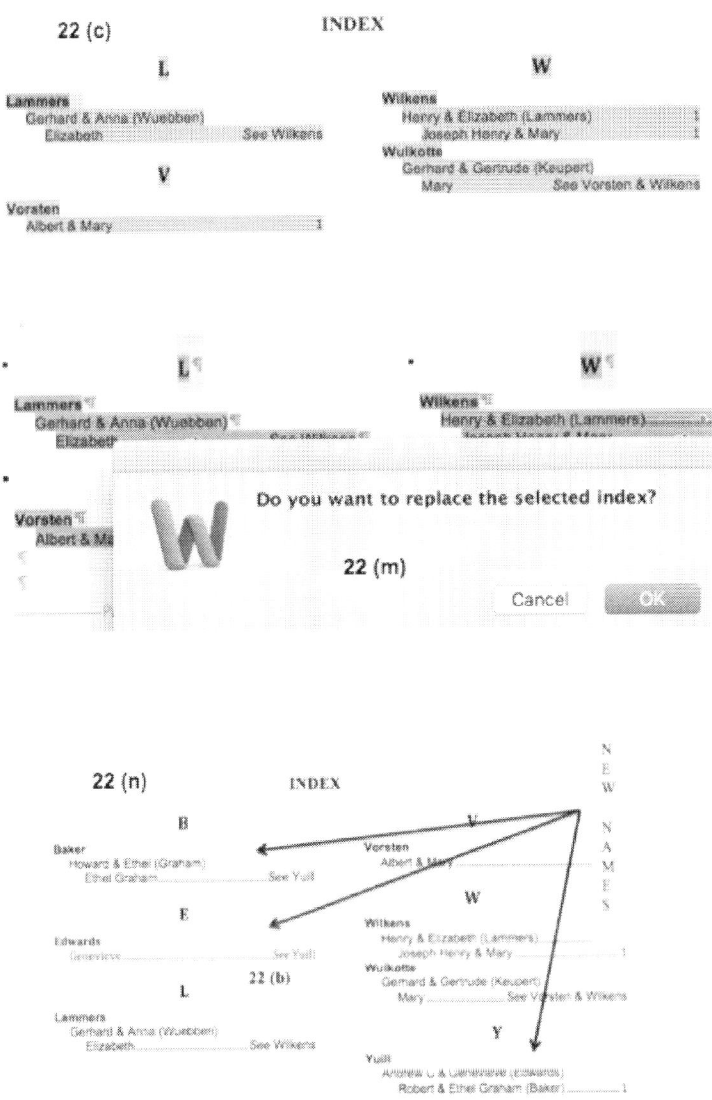

Figure 22 (m) and (n) - Example of Marked Entry Codes for New Names

Photographs, Newspapers, Records – Oh My

Now that you have the basics for setting up a Table of Contents, Table of Figures, an Index, etc. you may be thinking "if this is all there is to writing a book, then my book is going to look pretty boring to my readers". Well, actually there is more you can do to draw interest. You can add photographs, newspaper articles, documents; etc., which may help add substance, excitement, and enjoyment to your book. This chapter will help you learn how to add additional material to your book.

Before adding photographs, newspaper articles, documents, etc., (collectively referred to "pictures") to the book, it is important to scan the pictures to your computer using a dots-per-inch (DPI) resolution that will transfer to a quality output when the publisher prints the book. It is important to confirm the dpi with the publisher. I learned the hard way when I did not verify ahead of time the DPI the publisher needed, and I spent several days re-scanning all the pictures I planned to use in my book.

Since a JPEG format picture does not provide a quality image for printing, most publishers will require the pictures to be in a TIFF format as TIFF pictures provide the best quality image when printing. Publishers do not recommend JPEG format pictures because the JPEG file is a compressed file and it loses picture DPI quality each time it is opened and resaved.

The company Digital Memories has a great website which explains in depth the TIFF and JPEG formats along with the following chart which explains the pixel, file size and DPI.

How big will my files be?
This depends on the format they are saved to. The charts below list file sizes you can expect from TIFF and JPEG files.

35 MM FILM SCANNING: PIXEL & FILE SIZE OF A STANDARD 35MM FRAME

Scan Resolution	Pixel Dimensions	Megapixels	JPEG File Size	TIFF File Size
2000 DPI	2700 x 1800	4.8	2.2 MB - 3.8 MB	14.2 MB
3000 DPI	4050 x 2700	10.9	4.3 MB - 7.1 MB	32.0 MB
4000 DPI	5400 x 3600	19.4	6.7 MB - 10.8 MB	56.9 MB

* Based on 24 bit scanning and JPEG quality of 10 using Adobe Photoshop. JPEG file sizes vary.

35 MM FILM SCANNING: PIXEL & FILE SIZE OF A STANDARD 35MM FRAME

Scan Resolution	Pixel Dimensions	Megapixels	JPEG File Size	TIFF File Size
2000 DPI	2700 x 1800	4.8	2.2 MB - 3.8 MB	14.2 MB
3000 DPI	4050 x 2700	10.9	4.3 MB - 7.1 MB	32.0 MB
4000 DPI	5400 x 3600	19.4	6.7 MB - 10.8 MB	56.9 MB

* Based on 24 bit scanning and JPEG quality of 10 using Adobe Photoshop. JPEG file sizes vary.

300 DPI PRINT SCANS:

	Pixel Dimensions	JPEG File Size	TIFF File Size
3 X 5	900 x 1500	650 KB - 1 MB	3.9 MB
4 X 6	1200 x 1800	1.1 MB - 1.6 MB	6.3 MB
5 X 7	1500 x 2100	1.6 MB - 2.3 MB	9.2 MB
8 X 10	2400 x 3000	3.2 - 4.5 MB	21.2 MB

* Based on 24 bit scanning and JPEG quality of 10 using Adobe Photoshop. JPEG file sizes vary.

600 DPI PRINT SCANS:

	Pixel Dimensions	JPEG File Size	TIFF File Size
3 X 5	1800 x 3000	2.4 MB - 3.5 MB	15.8 MB
4 X 6	2400 x 3600	3.6 MB - 5.2 MB	25.3 MB
5 X 7	3000 x 4200	4.8 MB - 6.9 MB	36.9 MB
8 X 10	4800 x 6000	9.1 MB - 14.3 MB	84.4 MB

* Based on 24 bit scanning and JPEG quality of 10 using Adobe Photoshop. JPEG file sizes vary.

Permission granted by Robert C. Blau of Digital Memories on August 24, 2018.
http://www.digitalmemoriesonline.net

Figure 23 - Digital Memories - TIFF vs. JPEG Sizes

TIFF vs. JPEG

TIFF	JPEG
Tagged Image File Format	Joint Photographic Experts Group
Most widely supported file format	Most popular and compatible image format
Standard used by most commercial and professional printers	Supported by almost all of today's imaging software
No compression. 100% of data captured during scanning is retained	Compresses the file which causes the image data lose and affects the resolution
Large file size and not good for uploading to Internet or email	Smaller file sizes and best for uploading images to the Internet or email.
High resolution	Low resolution

Inserting Photographs and Documents

a) Place cursor on the page where the photo is to be inserted;

b) Select **Insert** on the Menu Bar and then select **Photo**;

c) Select the **File Location** of photo;

d) Select the photo or document to insert and then select **Insert**;

e) Selected photo or document is inserted on the page;
Note: a blue box with dots will appear around the figure or chart;

f) When the **Photo Tool Bar** appears; the photo or document can be (i) cropped, (ii) re-sized, (iii) formatted with a border, (iv) anchored to a specific place on the page, and (v) rotated.

Figure 24 - Picture Blue Line Frame

Figure 25 - Anchor Symbol for Photographs

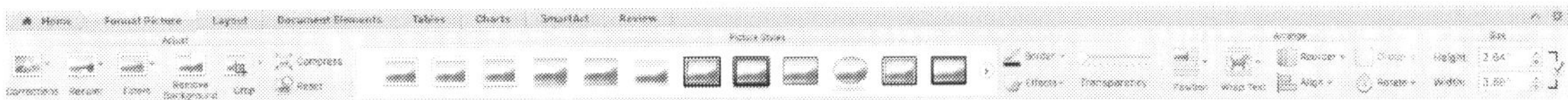

Figure 26 - Format Picture Tool Bar

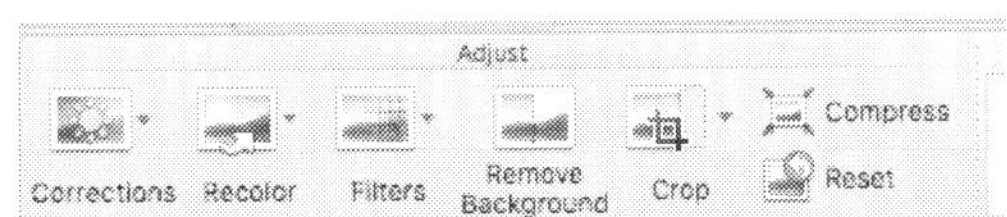

Figure 27 - Picture Adjustment Tool Bar

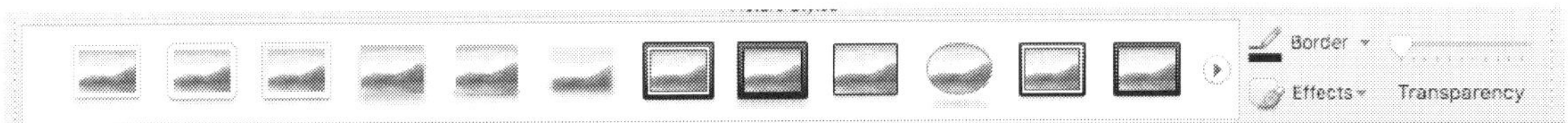

Figure 28 - Picture Border Tool Bar

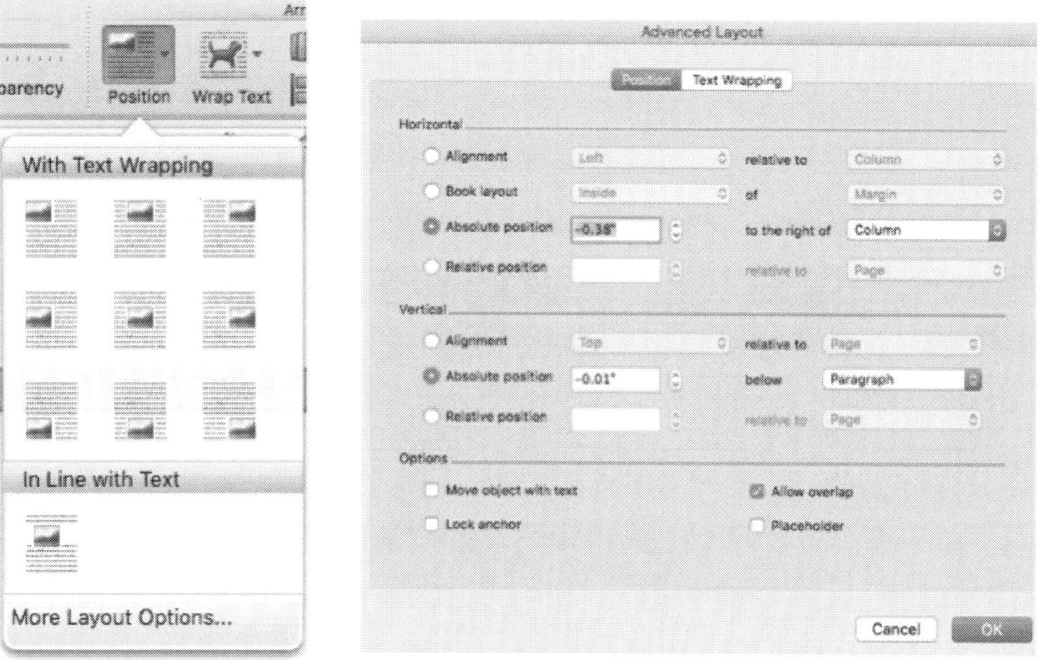

Figure 29 - Picture Position Button

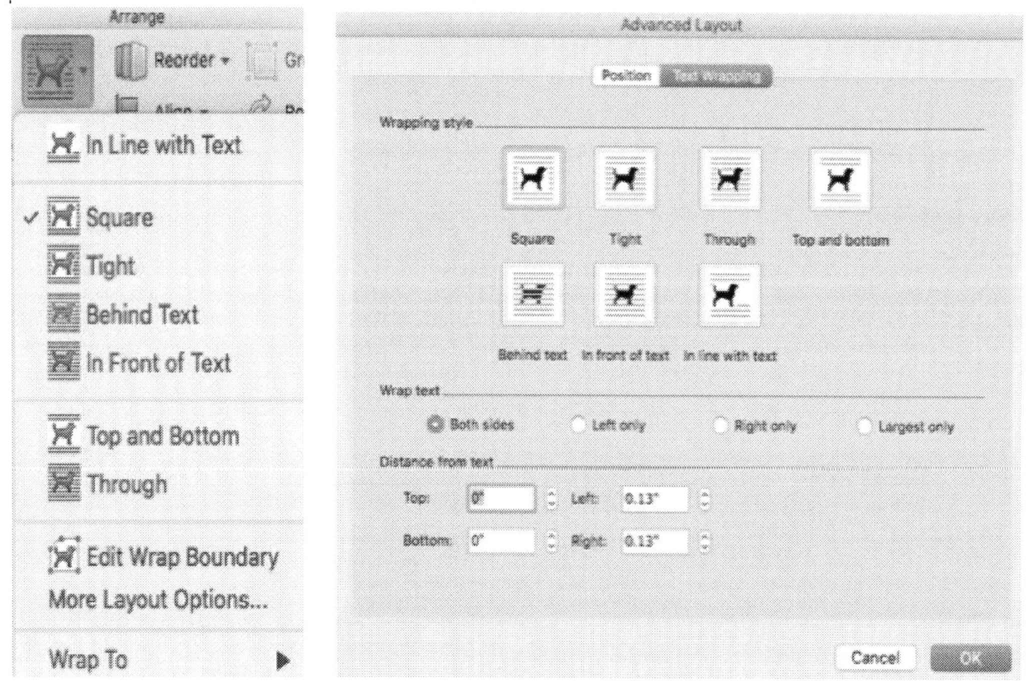

Figure 30 - Picture and Text Arrangement Button

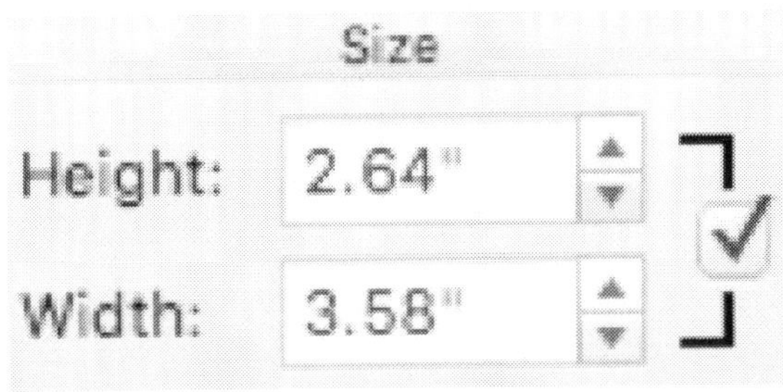

Figure 31 - Picture Sizing

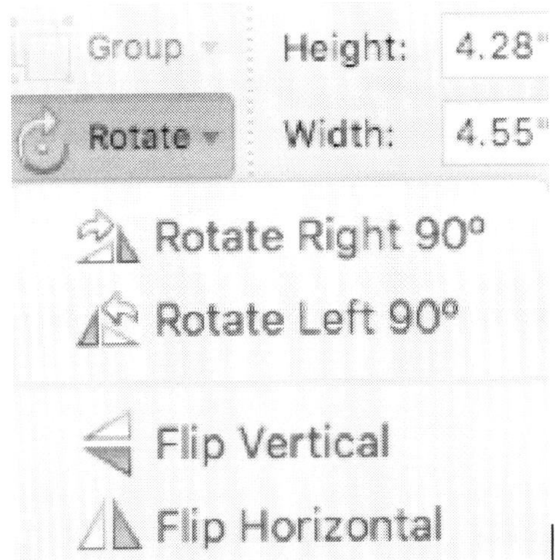

Figure 32 - Picture Rotation Button

Picture Cropping

a) Select the picture to be cropped
NOTE: blue line will frame the picture;

b) The **Format Picture Tool Bar** appears;

c) Select the **Picture Cropping Button**
Note: black lines will frame the corners and middle sections of the picture (see black circles on Figure 33);

d) Select the black line and move it until the picture is cropped to your liking (see Figure 33 for cropped picture).

Figure 33 - Picture Cropping (Original & Cropped)

Picture Borders

a) Select the picture to be formatted with a border
NOTE: blue line will frame the picture;

b) The **Format Picture Tool Bar** appears;

c) Review the **Picture Border** buttons

d) Select a border button and decide if the chosen border is to your liking;
NOTE: you can add color to your Borders by clicking on the down arrow on Border button;

e) When the **Color Palette** appears, choose a color for the border (see Figure 34 (e)); and

f) Select **Weights** to pick the thickness of the border (see Figure 34 (f)).

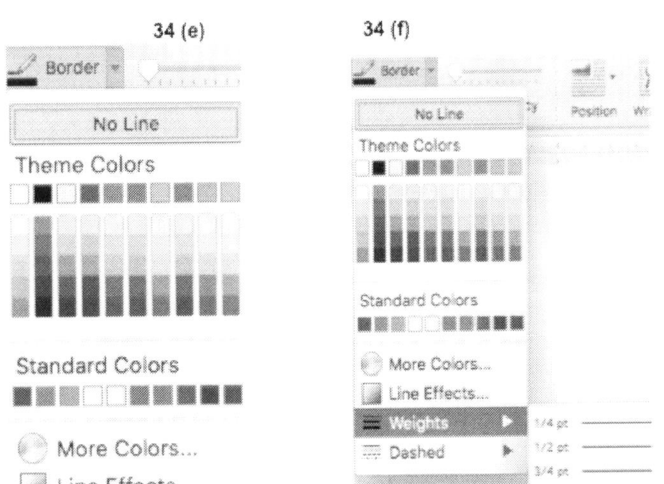

Figure 34 (a) through (f) - Border Examples and Color Palette

Examples of Picture Arrangements

NOTE: At times you may wish to arrange your pictures in a certain way. I have included an example of an arrangement that I used in my book.

Original Pictures for Picture Arrangement

Steps for Picture Arrangement

a) Select the picture that you wish to move forward
NOTE: blue line will frame the picture; (see Figure 24);

b) The **Format Picture Tool Bar** appears (see Figure 26);

c) Select the **Wrap Text** button in the **Arrange Tool Bar** section (see Figure 35 (c));

d) Select either **In Front of Text** or **Behind Text** from the drop-down fields;
*NOTE: (1) If the picture is to be moved in front of other pictures, click **In Front of Text** and the picture you selected will move to the front. For example, pictures (i) and (ii) must be changed so that picture (iii) can be fully displayed; (2) As there are three pictures to be corrected, steps (a) through (d) must also be completed for all pictures;* and

e) The final arrangement of the pictures appears.

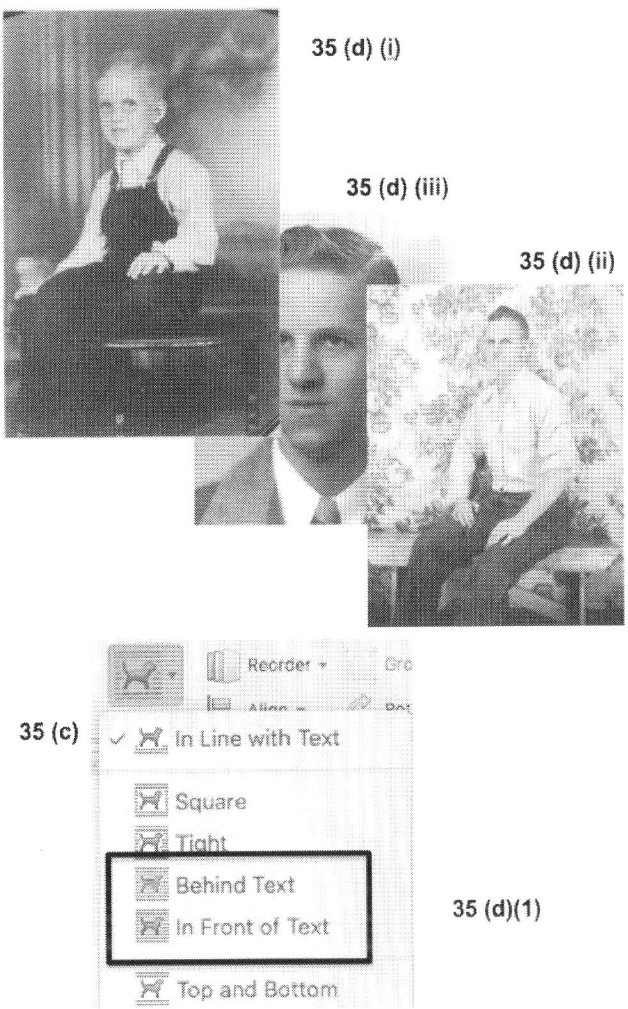

Figure 35 (c) through (c) - Picturc Arrangements

Final Arrangement of Pictures

NOTE: Positioning and anchoring the picture over each other completed the arrangement of the pictures.

Figure 35 (e) - Final Arrangement of Pictures

CHAPTER 6: WRITING THE STORY

My mom was one of the original genealogy searchers. She began her family genealogy research in 1948 when her high school English teacher gave the students the option to read a book and prepare a book report or prepare a family history paper. Luckily, mom chose the family history assignment. From 1948 to present time, mom added birth, marriages and death information to her family history paper. Mom remembers and told me many times that she had to resolve many family disputes over a birth, marriage or death when her mother would call up and say "get your family history out and put your thinking hat on because we have another dispute to resolve".

As for myself, I still say my mom conned me into this genealogy stuff and gave me the genealogy bug. This is one time I can actually blame mom for something. But, I love that she got me addicted to genealogy! Mom and I have had a lot of fun traveling and researching for those elusive genealogy records.

I still remember the month and year that mom got me into genealogy. It was October 1987 while on a trip to visit my mom's brother and other relatives in Iowa. While in her hometown of Cresco, Iowa, mom stated she wished she could find her mother and father's birth and marriage records along with her grandparents' birth, marriage and death records. My return response to her was "no problem, that is what I went to college for and I will show you how to find the records." Upon finding the appropriate records, I asked mom why she wanted all these records and her response was to push the family history notebook to me. Once I looked at her notebook, I said, "along with the vital records, why not get newspaper articles, church records, etc.", and her response was "I don't know how" and I told her I would show her how to obtain the other records. She grinned because she knew she had me hooked.

When mom and I discovered that we were the only ones searching the entire Carolan family line, i.e., aunts, uncles, and cousins along with collateral lines of these ancestors we knew we had to find a way to preserve the family history and to share it with other family members, and we began to kick around the idea of doing a family history book. After our genealogy trip to Ireland, we decided it was time to start drafting the family history book.

While I started the writing process, mom worked on verifying and organizing all the genealogy information we had collected over the years. I think I gave the easy task to mom, because the writing task while exciting also had problems. The problems included writers block, trying to make the first writing perfect, and family organization.

The first problem we solved was the organization of ancestors. We decide to start the book out with the most distant ancestors and their children and follow with the next generation and then the future generations. We also decided to organize each family by order of birth.

The second, problem got solved by sitting at the computer and just type. I decided that the first writing did not have to be perfect. It was more important to get ideas done and cleanup later.

As for the third problem, having writer's block came and went as I was drafting. Everyone has writers block some time, but the trick is to find a way to get back on tract with your writing. One of my tricks was to listen to my favorite music and another one was to have a notepad with me so that I could jot down my thoughts and ideas as they came to me. There were several times that an idea would come to me just as I was falling asleep. I didn't want to lose the idea so I would write it on the notepad hoping I would be able to read my scribbling in the morning.

Some Tips and Tricks to Start Writing

- Relax;
- Start small and become familiar with the writing and publishing concept;
- Just type and don't worry about sentence structure until later;
- Listen to your favorite music;
- Jot down ideas as they come to you; and
- Have fun.

Since you are familiar with the family you are writing about and having been the researcher, reviewer and organizer of the genealogy information collected over the years, you will be able to write a great story.

If you are still having trouble getting your thoughts down on paper, I recommend you think like a journalist. If you review any newspaper article, hopefully the journalist followed the 6Ws rule when writing the newspaper article.

The 6Ws rules are (i) who, (2) what, (3) when, (4) where, (5) how, and (6) why. The 6Ws are like a formula for getting a complete story on a subject; therefore, once the formula is completed, the answers from the 6Ws will enable you to write your story.[8]

Some Helpful Questions Using the 6Ws:

- Who was involved? or Who did it?
- What happened?
- Where did it happen?
- When did it take place?
- Why did it happen?
- How did it happen

Each question should have a factual answer. These facts will help you complete the story. When asking questions, it is best to use open-ended questions because open-ended questions require more thought and more than a simple one-word answer. The opposite of open-ended questions are closed-ended which requires just a "yes" or "no" answer and are not very helpful when writing a story.

Now lets take a look at a document to see if we can find the 6Ws.

Finding the 6Ws

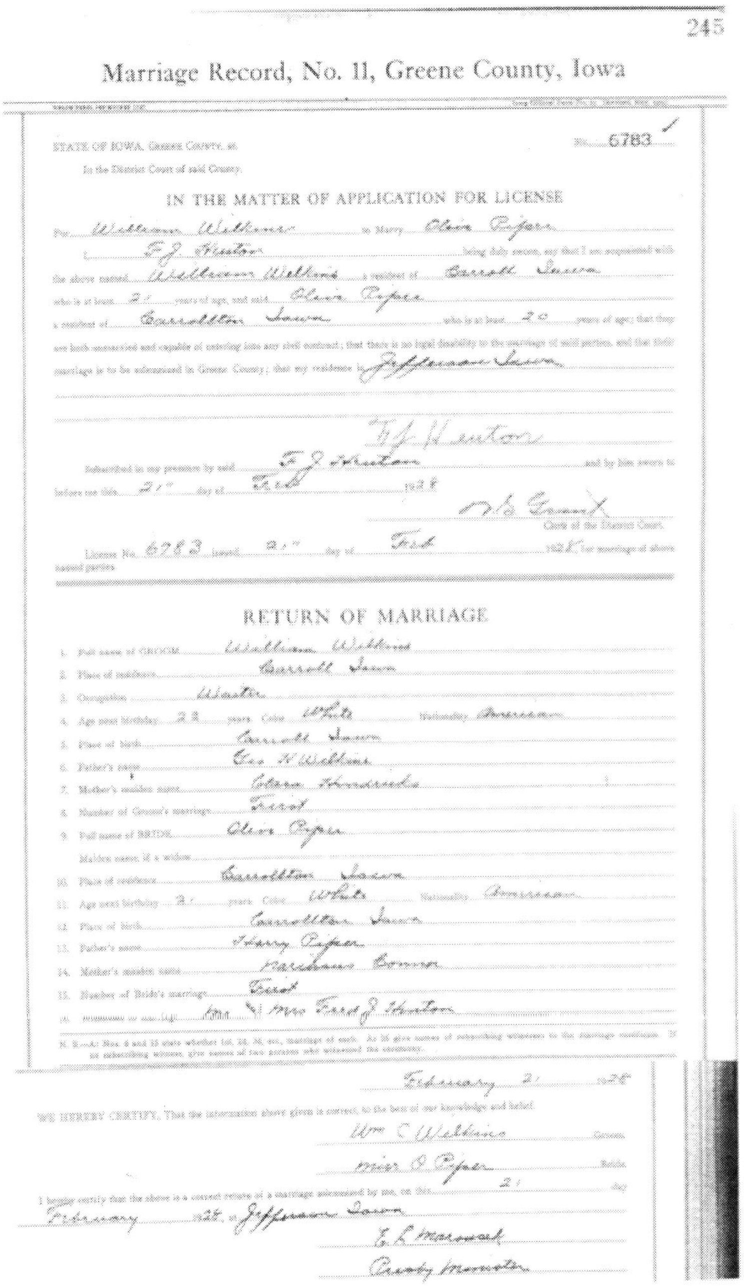

245

Marriage Record, No. 11, Greene County, Iowa

STATE OF IOWA, Greene County, ss.

In the District Court of said County.

No. 6783

IN THE MATTER OF APPLICATION FOR LICENSE

RETURN OF MARRIAGE

WE HEREBY CERTIFY, That the information above given is correct, to the best of our knowledge and belief.

Wm C Wilkins

Miss O Piper

Figure 36 - Marriage Record - The 6Ws

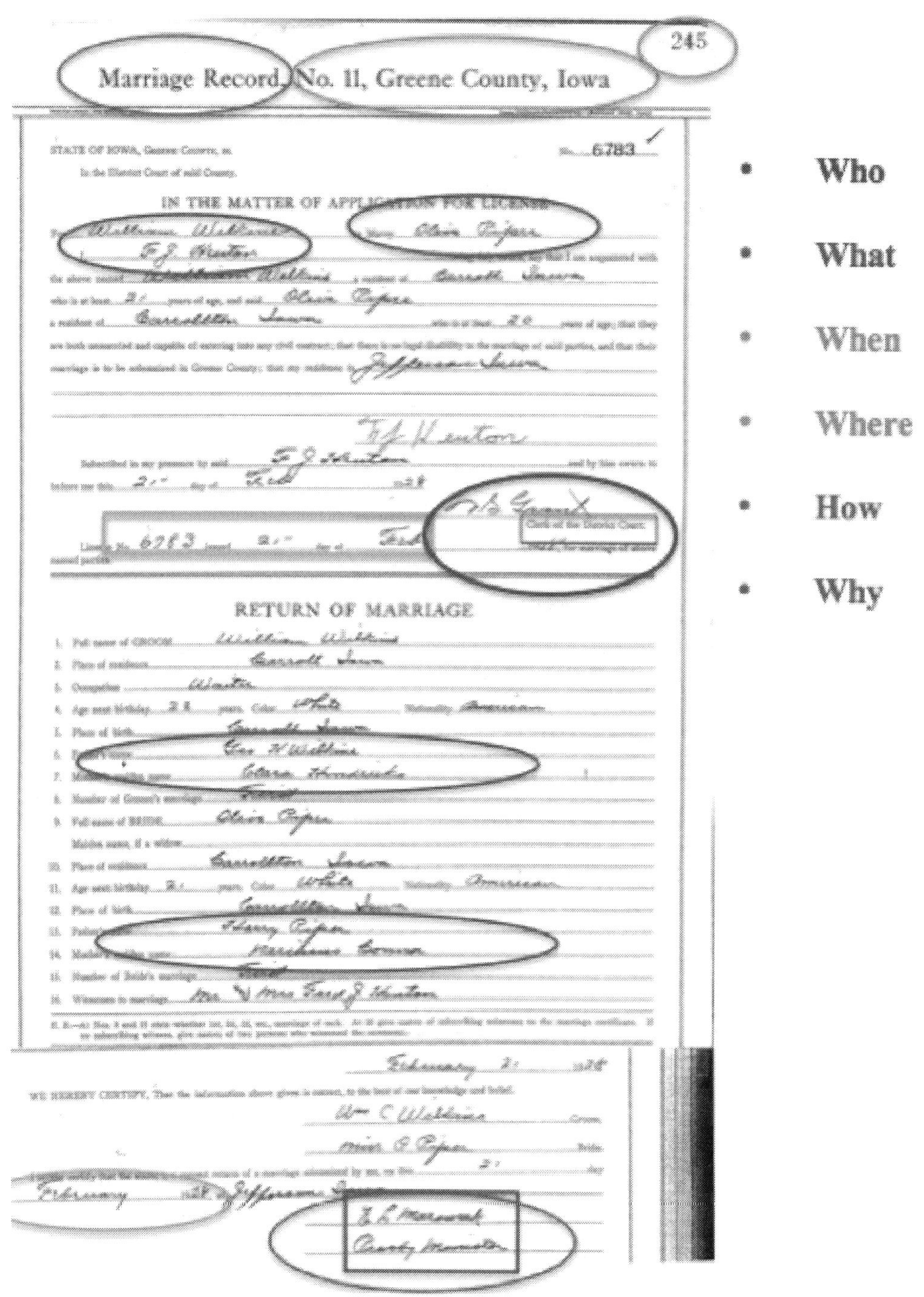

245

Marriage Record, No. 11, Greene County, Iowa

No. 6783

IN THE MATTER OF APPLICATION FOR LICENSE

RETURN OF MARRIAGE

Figure 37 - Marriage Record - The 6Ws Highlighted

As you can see, a document may have several 6Ws that can be used to write your story.

After analyzing the document and finding all of the 6Ws, let's take a closer look at the document to see what can be written about the information.

Obvious Information

- Bride & Groom
- Witnesses
- Residence of wedding party
- Dates
- Ages
- Service performed by
- Source information
- Parents
- Location of wedding

My Write-up using the obvious information.

> At the ripe old age of 21 my grandfather William Wilkens married my 20-year-old grandmother Oliver Piper at Jefferson, Iowa on February 21, 1928 by the Presbyterian Minister E. L. Marsoucek. When William and Olive decided to obtain their marriage license, they were required to provide a witness who was acquainted with the prospective bride and groom and could affirm that they were of legal age. Their witness was F. J. Heuton who is a brother-in-law to Olive. Olive's parents are ... Luckily Iowa required all marriage records to be filed in the county clerks office, which allowed me to find my grandparents marriage information and obtain a copy of their record from Marriage Record Book 11, Page 245, Greene County, Iowa and referred to as marriage license number 6783.

If you notice in my write-up example, the Why is missing, but by using the photographs below the Why is evident

WHY

Wedding Day

50th Anniversary

60th Anniversary

Figure 38 - 6Ws WHY

Now let's think outside the box and think about the information not found in the document. Using the 6Ws rule, what are some of the non-obvious information?

Not so Obvious

a) **Events Leading Up to Wedding**
   i. What celebrations occurred once the engagement was announced?
b) **Bride's & Groom's Relationship to Witnesses**
   i. Who are the witnesses?
   ii. How are they related to the bride and groom?
c) **Weather**
   i. What was the weather like on the day they got married?
d) **Gifts**
   i. How many gifts did they receive?
   ii. What did they receive?
   iii. Who gave them the gifts?
e) **Wedding Colors**
   i. What were the wedding colors?
f) **Parents**
   i. Who are the parents of the bride and groom?
g) **Honeymoon**
   i. Where was the honeymoon?
h) **Wedding Cake**
   i. What did the wedding cake look like?
   ii. Who made the wedding cake?
i) **Wedding Reception**
   i. Where was the wedding reception held?
   ii. What did they have at the wedding reception?

The not so obvious information can provide additional information to write. For example, when my father and mother were married, my mother's aunt made the wedding cake and served the wedding breakfast. In addition, my mother's cousin, son to the aunt who made the wedding cake, designed and helped make the wedding gown.

Don't sweat it if you do not have information regarding the non-obvious information as you can research the customs during your ancestor's timeframe as they may have followed same customs. For example, you may have to state something like:

> *During the 1880s, the custom for marriage ceremonies was … I am not sure if my ancestor followed the 1880 customs …*

By analyzing documents using the 6Ws, your story will fall into place. Here is an analysis of a census record using the 6Ws.

As you can see, your story will develop if the 6Ws rule is used when reviewing your documents.

Figure 39 - Additional Example for the 6Ws

The book does not have to be just about the documents you found during your research. Once again, you should think "outside the box" for generating your family stories. In my book, *Climbing the Irish Shamrock*, I included chapters about the Irish cottage my ancestor lived in before immigrating to America, and the church they established in Decorah, Iowa. The cottage and church stories explain the life my ancestors had before immigration and what was important to them after immigration to America.

Other Out of the Box Ideas

- Other family members
- Special holidays & vacations
- Family home
- Military service
- Education
- Family heirlooms
- Hobbies & occupations
- Letters
- Recipes

Family Heirlooms

Other Family Members

Yes, there is a story for each one of these photographs. From the dog that bit me every time I tried to feed her to how my dad solved the problem.

And yes, one of our family members was a pony. A lot of children wish for a pony, and I think my sister, Susie had a special type of pull, because we ended up with a pony after it was won in a drawing. We had a lot of fun with the pony.

As you are preparing your book and writing your book, you should be searching for a publishing company that will be able to print your book. As mentioned in Chapter 2, it is important to reach out to publishing companies to obtain their publishing requirements such as page margins, photographs, printing cost, etc. Let's take a look at how to find publishing companies and what they can do for you.

CHAPTER 7: PUBLISHING THE BOOK

There are several sources available for finding a publishing company. Publishing companies can be found be checking genealogy sources such as books, magazines and genealogy societies. Other places to look for publishing companies are websites, yellow pages, and published writers. When searching for the right publishing company, you should research and select a publisher that can provide the following:

Coaching

- Publisher should offer coaching by phone, in-person, email and/or snail mail. And you should also be able to contact the publisher in the same manner.
- Publisher should be willing to provide referrals of previous customers so that you can speak to them and determine what their experience was like in using the publisher. My publisher provided a few customer names, and I was able to discuss the publisher with them to determine if they had a good experience with the publisher.

Design and Proof Suggestions

- Publisher should be willing to review a sampling of your pages for your book to ensure their printing process will produce a quality book.
- Publisher should be willing to discuss and suggest book cover designs along with the type of binding to use and the differences.
- Writer should have the right to check and proof the book cover, title page, and copyright page before the book is published.
- Publisher should assist with the title page and the copyright page. I elected to have my publisher file the necessary copyright documents as they have the expertise for filing a copyright application.

Sample Book

- A sample of a publisher's previous printed job will help determine the publisher's ability to handle your print job.
- A library is a great source to review books to determine a style that you want for your book.
- Inform your publisher about the likes and dislikes about the sample books you reviewed.

Acid-free paper

- Acid-free paper is the best for preservation of your book.
- The publisher should be willing to use acid-free paper.

Provide an estimated cost for print job

- Publisher should provide a cost estimate for the print job.
- Publisher should be willing to provide ideas for cutting costs, if needed. For example, color printing can cost more. Plus, sometimes the more books printed are cheaper; therefore, if more is cheaper it is best to receive payment upfront from everyone wanting a book.
- Publisher should explain the cost for each item needed to print your book. For example, (a) the cost of a hardbound book vs. a paperback book; or (b) offset print vs. camera ready.

Provides a contract specifying the terms and obligations between the parties

- Publisher should provide a contract for your review and signature before any printing job starts.
- If you do not understand the terms and obligations under the contract, contact an attorney.
- Remember, most lawsuits occur because one or both parties did not have an understanding of the job to be done, i.e., the scope of work the publisher is to preform and what the writer is to provide.

Marketing Ideas

- Publisher may or may not be able to assist in marketing your book.
- It is the writer's choice whether to sell or give away the book for free.
- If you do elect to sell your book, the publisher may or may not collect the payments for the book sells. If the publisher handles, the publisher may want a percentage of the book sells.

***NOTE**: When I elected to sell my book, the writer I interviewed during my research for a publisher gave me great advice. Per the writer, she recommended getting payment up upfront because her family members ordered books with a promise to pay, but her family members did not pay and she was stuck with several boxes of books.*

Select your publisher carefully as you worked hard on writing the book and the output should be a quality printed book from your publisher. During your search for a publishing company you may hear various printing styles such as desktop publishing, offset printing, and print-on-demand. Each of these printing styles deal with how you and the publisher will print out your book.

Printing Styles

Desktop Publishing

- Use of personal computer.
- Allows writer the freedom to use different fonts, margins, embed illustrations and graphs directly into document.
- Combines a personal computer and WYSIWYG (what you see is what you get).

Offset Printing

- Use of metal plate, which transfers the image to another surface, i.e., rubber blanket, then applied to paper.
- Equipment and set-up costs are high, but the actual printing process is relatively inexpensive.

Print On-Demand (POD)

- Uses a digital printing process.
- Buyers purchase the book when they want and book is only printed when an order is made.
- Writers and publishers do not have to spend a lot of money upfront.
- Select a POD publisher that meets your needs.

Print-on-Demand Book Services

- Amazon Kindle Direct Publishing
- Lulu
- Blurb
- Lightning Source

CHAPTER 8: Publishing Terms

Book Covers

- **Paperback**: Stapled or "perfect bound" (glued)
- **Hardback**: Stitched Cloth pasted over binder's boards

Camera-Ready

- Manuscript is ready to go to press.
- Prepared in such a way that it is ready for photographing prior to being made into a printing plate.

Contract/Publishing Agreement

- Contract specifies the rights of the parties: (i) copyright grants; (ii) author's and publisher's respective obligations under the agreement; and (iii) compensation.

Copyright

- The exclusive right to reproduce and distribute works of original expression in a fixed format such as a story or creating a work of art.

Desktop Publishing

- Computer generated / digital manuscript.
- Allows writer the freedom to use different fonts, margins, embed illustrations and graphs directly into document.
- Combines a computer and WYSIWYG (what you see is what you get)

Drop Folios

- A page number located at the bottom of a page.
- Publisher and Editors may refer to drop folios as page number

Grayscale

- Photos, paintings and illustrations in black and white instead of color.

Joint Photographic Experts Group (JPG or JPEG)

- JPEG; see **Photographs, Newspapers, Records – Oh My** above.

Line Art

- Strictly black and white images.

Line-Editing/Copy Editing

- Line-by-line editing of a manuscript concentrating on style, punctuation, spelling, grammar, flow, sequencing, clarity, consistency, and content errors.

Manuscript

- An author's written material before it is typeset and printed.

Offset Printing

- Use of metal plate, which transfers the image to another surface, i.e., rubber blanket, then applied to paper.
- Equipment and set-up costs are high, but the actual printing process is relatively inexpensive.

Print On-Demand (POD)

- Uses a digital printing process.
- Buyers purchase the book when they want and book is only printed when an order is made.
- Writers and publishers do not have to spend a lot of money upfront.
- Select a POD publisher that meets your needs.

Proofreading

- A final proofing of the book and usually focused on cleaning up any typographical errors before the manuscript is typeset.

Tagged Image File Format

- TIFF; see **Photographs, Newspapers, Records – Oh My** above.

WYSIWYG

- "What You See Is What You Get"

To see additional publishing terms, the Book Jobs website has a very extensive listed of publishing terms at http://www.bookjobs.com/commonly-used-terms

CHAPTER 9: MARKETING THE BOOK

If you elect to sell your book to family or the general public, you need to think about how you plan to market your book and/or notify your family or the public about your book. You should figure out the most cost effective way to reach your audience.

When I elected to sell my book to family members, I searched for the best way to locate family members. I used several marketing methods, including, social media, newspaper, snail mail, etc. As social media avenues open up, you will have more ways to find and reach out to people.

My marketing methods included:

- Organizing a family reunion
- Facebook
- Email
- Contacting the local newspaper in the town where your relatives live or lived is a great way to find distant relatives far and wide. People subscribe to their hometown paper so they can stay in touch with family, friends and hometown events.
- As the publisher provided a cost estimate for the printing process, I was able to determine the approximate price for the book to cover the print cost.

Most people are very understanding about the expense for printing a book, but some people will never be happy and all I could do was explain the hotel, meal and copying costs, and time for doing the research throughout the years.

CHAPTER 10: EXAMPLES OF GRAYSCALE AND LINE ART

Examples of Grayscale and Line Art

Grayscale

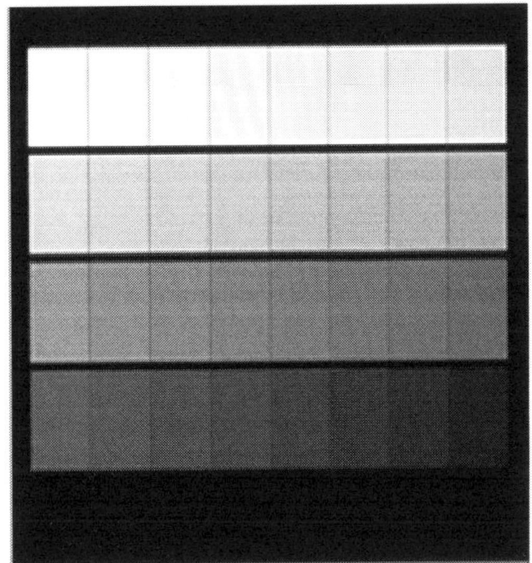

Figure 40 - Grayscale and Line Art

Line Art

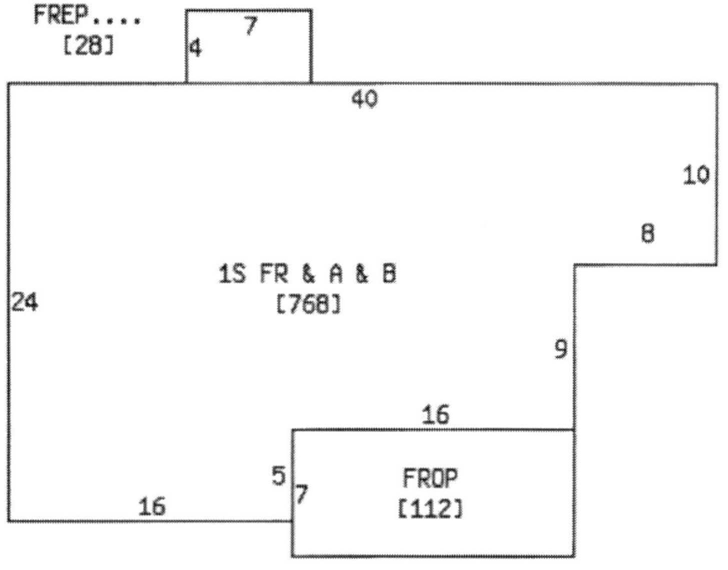

Grayscale/Halftone

These are examples of Grayscale/Halftone because of lines and shading.

BIBLIOGRAPHY

Hatcher, Patricia Law, CG, *Producing a Quality Family History*. Salt Lake City: Ancestry Incorporated, 1996.

McClure, Rhonda R., *Digitizing Your Family History*. Cincinnati: Family Tree Books, 2004.

Mills, Elizabeth Shown, CG, CGL, FASG, FNGS, *Evidence! Citation & Analysis for the Family Historian*. Baltimore: Genealogical Publishing Company.

Szucs, Loretto Dennis and Sandra Hargreaves Luebking, editors. *The Source: A Guidebook of American Genealogy*. Salt Lake City: Ancestry Incorporated, 1997.

Board for Certification of Genealogists, *The BCG Genealogical Standards Manual*, Ancestry Incorporated, 2000 and 2014.

University of Chicago Press, *The Chicago Manual of Style*, 16th Edition, 2010.

Finley, Carmen J., *Creating a Winning Family History*, National Genealogical Society, Arlington, VA, 2010.

ADDITIONAL RESOURCES FOR WRITERS

Alzo, Lisa, *Research, Write, Connect!* https://www.researchwriteconnect.com/

Vigeant, Meghan, *Stories To Tell* https://storiestotell.net

PRODUCTION NOTES

1. The software used in creating this book is Microsoft Word for Mac 2001, version 14.7.7 ("Word Mac "). While this book was written using a MacBook Pro computer and Word Mac, the steps used with the Word Mac can be followed using a PC computer program running Microsoft Word. In addition, you may wish to research the Internet and YouTube to find and use additional techniques for writing and publishing your book.

2. Permission to use the Microsoft screen shots granted by the Microsoft Corporation ("Microsoft") via email received from Microsoft dated October 12, 2018 at 7:00 pm

   Microsoft email statement: "*Microsoft Corporation grants you permission to use screen shots of Microsoft's product screens in your educational publication Preparing to Write and Publish Your Book: Tips and Tricks for the Writer provided in your October 5, 2018 email."*

   Below are the guidelines for using altered screen shots:

   - *Do not use screen shots that contain any third-party content.*
   - *Do not use screen shots that contain an image of an identifiable individual.*
   - *If your use includes references to a Microsoft product, you must use the full name of the product. When referencing any Microsoft trademarks, follow the General Microsoft Trademark Guidelines.*
   - *You must include the following statement: "Used with permission from Microsoft."*
   - *Your use may not be obscene or pornographic, and you may not be disparaging, defamatory, or libelous to Microsoft, any of its products, or any other person or entity.*
   - *A separate request is required to use the screen shots for any use or distribution not described in your email. There is no permission fee for this use.*

   Best regards,

   Microsoft Permissions"

ABOUT THE AUTHOR

I'm Regina Yuill, the genealogy enthusiast in my family and author of ***Preparing to Write and Publish Your Book: Tips and Tricks for the Writer***. My concept for a family history book began many years ago after several genealogy adventures with my mother. After adding more genealogy records to my mother's genealogy collection (which she had started in 1948), I began to wonder how we were going to preserve all the genealogy records and family knowledge we had gathered.

Little did I realize the daunting project I was about to begin. I had limited experience with preparing indexes, table of contents, footnotes, endnotes, photographs and plain old writing techniques. So I decided to attend genealogy society meetings and national genealogy conferences to learn more about the writing and publishing process. However, as I soon discovered, there was a lack of writing and publishing guidebooks geared towards genealogists and family historians. Despite this, I decided to jump in with both feet forward and published my first family history book in 2005.

And as any proud author would do, I'm always happy to show my book to fellow genealogists in the hopes that I can encourage them to preserve their own family history by also writing a book. I'm a firm believer in the preservation of history and have given lectures explaining tips and tricks on writing and publishing a book.

Even with these lectures, I realized that many genealogists were still struggling with their writing and publishing projects. So, I decided to write ***Preparing to Write and Publish Your Book: Tips and Tricks for the Writer***, which explains the tips and tricks I used in preparing my own book. I hope my book will make the writing and publishing process easier as you prepare your own family history book.

Good luck, have fun and I hope you succeed in publishing a family history book for others to enjoy.

ENDNOTES

[1] Hussein, Radiyyah, "What is a Realist? How to Tell if You Have a Realist Personality." Article. *CogniFit Health, Brain & Neuroscience*. https://blog.cognifit.com/what-is-a -realist-8-signs-to-tell-if-you-have-a-realist-personality/ : posted 29 March 2018.

[2] Wikimedia Foundation, Inc., "Life Expectancy." Website. *Wikipedia The Free Encyclopedia*. https://en.wikipedia.org/wiki/Life_expectancy : posted 3 September 2018.

[3] Wikimedia Foundation, Inc., "To Tell the Truth." Website. *Wikipedia The Free Encyclopedia*. https://en.wikipedia.org/wiki/To_Tell_the_Truth : posted 5 September 2018.

[4] Lafreniere, Luke, "What are Fonts and Typefaces?" YouTube. *Techquickie*. https://www.youtube.com/watch?v=l2iNthl-RUk : posted 27 May 2016.

[5] United States Patent and Trademark Office (USPTO), "General information concerning patents." Website. *Inventor Resources*. https://www.uspto.gov/patents-getting-started/general-information-concerning-patents : posted 14 March 2018.

[6] Wikimedia Foundation, Inc., "Copyright." Website. *Wikipedia The Free Encyclopedia*. https://en.wikipedia.org/wiki/Copyright : posted 5 September 2018.

[7]WikiHow, Inc., "How to Dedicate a Book." Website. *WikeHow to do anything*." https://www.wikihow.com/Dedicate-a-Book : posted 24 August 2018.

[8] Spencer-Thomas, Owen. "Press release: getting the facts straight." Article. *Owen Spencer-Thomas*. https://www.owenspencer-thomas.com/journalism/media-tips/writing-a-press-release : posted 24 February 2012.

29726801R00061

Made in the USA
Lexington, KY
03 February 2019